I0532781

MY LIFE AS A
STUDIO WIFE

A Lifetime of Love and Music with Bruce Swedien

BEA SWEDIEN

Westviking Press

Ocala, FL

Also by Bea Swedien: Under the Red Blanket, MX Publishing, 2011

Westviking Press
Ocala, FL

PHOTO CREDITS:
Bruce Swedien, Bea Swedien, Roberta Swedien, Bengt Anderson, Ellsworth Swedien, Louise Swedien, Steve Wiese, Maury Phillips/Getty Images, Erik Nuri, Mike Vye, Gareth Maynard, Bjorn Asplind.

Publisher's Note: Every effort has been made to trace copyright holders and to obtain their permission for the use of copyright material. The publisher apologizes for any errors or omissions and would be grateful if notified of any corrections that should be incorporated in future reprints or editions of this book.

Edited by Howard Massey
Book Layout © 2017 BookDesignTemplates.com
Cover design by Mario Lampic

My Life As a Studio Wife / Bea Swedien. -- 1st ed.
ISBN: 979-8-218-68379-5
eBook ISBN: 979-8-218-68381-8

Library of Congress Control Number: 2025914360

For Bruce, my best friend and the love of my life.

Special thanks to Roberta Swedien, Howard Massey, and Travis Atria.

CONTENTS

Foreword by Quincy Jones i

Introduction by Roberta Swedien iii

Preface by Bea Swedien... v

CHILDHOODS.. 1

MINNEAPOLIS.. 17

CHICAGO 31

LOS ANGELES.. 71

CONNECTICUT 149

FLORIDA 167

Acknowledgments.. 197

Index 199

Foreword

BY QUINCY JONES

I was always pleased that Bea had just the right amount of "Ghetto," which is why she is such a 360 degree person. This book gives an insight into one of the most irrepressible, high-spirited people I know.

There are not enough words to express how much Bruce meant to me. He was my dear friend and brother, he was without question the absolute best engineer in the business, and for more than 50 years I wouldn't even think about going into a recording session unless I knew Bruce was behind the board. Bruce was the guru of engineers. We recorded more albums together than I can remember, from Dinah and Basie in Chicago in the 50s to the Brothers Johnson and Michael [Jackson], and I can't imagine recording one of those albums without him. We are forever connected spiritually, mentally and physically, and he deserved every honor and adulation that was bestowed upon him.

Along with the late great Rod Temperton, we reached heights that we could have never imagined and made history together. I have always said it's no accident that more than four decades later, no matter where I go in the world, in every club, like clockwork at the witching hour you hear "Billie Jean," "Beat It," "Wanna Be Starting Something," and "Thriller." That was the sonic genius of Bruce Swedien, and to this day I can hear artists trying to replicate him. I called him "Svensk," which means Swedish man, and I will cherish every moment we shared together laughin', lovin', livin', and givin'.

That being said, Bea was Bruce's north star. Without her in his life, none of his accomplishments would have mattered as much to him. That is how much he loved and cherished her.

Introduction

BY ROBERTA SWEDIEN

Growing up, I assumed everyone's father worked all hours of the day and night and sometimes into the next morning with the greatest musicians in the world, and everyone's mother had faced down a tiger. It wasn't until much later that I realized how rare and unique life was with Bruce and Bea Swedien.

I spent my formative years in the Chicago studios, mostly Universal Recording on Rush and Walton. Studio A was a huge, two-story room strewn with chairs, microphone stands, cables, music stands, ashtrays, and old, cold coffee in paper cups sitting on a somewhat battered but resonant Steinway. The control room was a dark cave with hundreds of tiny lights and yellow meters with jumping needles. The music was everything from jazz to big band to jingles. The musicians were often quiet guys—intense, calm, experienced, ready to play anything masterfully at any time. Some of them took me under their wing. I was the young musician kid, hanging with my engineer dad at work after my weekly piano lesson at the Chicago Conservatory of Music. Some of those guys were members of the renowned Chicago Symphony Orchestra. Their virtuosity and precision were unforgettable. I thought everyone played like that.

Often my mom was there with home-made treats, a stunning smile, and a story or two. Everyone loved her. She had been in studios with my dad since she was eighteen. It was a second home. For all of us.

From her I learned about adventure and the wide world out there. I grew up hearing her childhood stories of India: headhunter tribals, tigers on the verandah, scary jungle ghosts, dusty train rides across the country, and the madcap antics of her wild brothers that involved spears and banana trees. What I learned from both of my parents was, "Go for it, no matter what. Be brave, trust your gut and use your brain."

These worlds merged for me when I went to India. I taught music at my mother's old boarding school, learned the tabla, played Rachmaninoff in concert, spoke Hindi, rafted on the Ganges, conducted the Mozart Requiem, abandoned cutlery and ate curried rice with my piano fingers.

Classical, popular, East, West—they all worked together. In a way, I was living a lesson from my parents' uncommon life together: There are no boundaries. Not in music. Not in life.

For my parents, there were no boundaries in love, either. Their love began literally before my mother's birth, and it endures after my father's death. It stretched across decades, homes, musics, countries. It survived pressures that would surely have broken most people. In a way, it is the most unlikely, wonderful part of their unlikely, wonderful story.

This book is a tribute to that love.

Preface

BY BEA SWEDIEN

Before we left for Japan for the start of the second leg of the Bad Tour in early 1988, Bruce and I joined Michael Jackson and all the musicians and dancers for rehearsals at an indoor arena in Pensacola, Florida. The sound truck was driven from Los Angeles. It was the same crew that had worked with us on Lena Horne's Broadway show. During one of the rehearsals in this large, empty basketball arena, I found a folding chair and placed it in the center of the basketball court. It was incredible to be the only member of the audience. When the rehearsal was over I yelled and applauded. Michael yelled back, "That's gotta be Bea!"

"Don't ever bring your wife to the studio," Bruce had been warned by other engineers. Fortunately for me, he ignored their advice. Bruce always included me. He didn't follow the crowd in any way, not in his recording, not in his lifestyle. Then again, I was a young Swedish-American blonde with crazy, entertaining stories about headhunters in India. Not the average wife. Plus, I understood Bruce's job, and I understood what the musicians were there to do. Most people might think it would be boring and tedious to listen to many takes of the same piece of music, but it was never boring to me or anyone else in the control room. I understood the studio. I had seen one being built. I was, to put it in the parlance of the times, one of the guys.

Bruce absolutely loved what he did. And I loved it too: all the tracks of each and every album. He'd come home, we'd go into our studio and he'd play what they'd been working on that day. Each track was new, innovative and memorable. It was always so exciting to be right there, a part of this, as it was happening.

For a long time, people have been telling me to write a book. A second book. The first one, *Under the Red Blanket*, was about growing up in the jungles of northeast India amongst headhunter tribes, snakes and tigers. (I always said that prepared me for dealing with record company executives.) Now it's time to tell the story of my equally uncommon life with my husband and best friend, Bruce Swedien. In our 67 years together, Bruce and I seemed to hurtle headlong from one adventure to the next while he was making a name for himself as one of the most important and influential audio engineers ever. Most wives would never go into the studio—if they were even invited, which as a rule they weren't. But I did, and Bruce loved having me there as much as I loved being there.

Over the years, I watched some of the biggest stars in music create their greatest hits. I was there in the 1950s with Dinah Washington and Oscar Peterson, and in the 1960s with Duke Ellington and Frankie Valli and the Four Seasons, and in all the decades to come, with all the great music to come, from Ramsey Lewis to the Chi-Lites, from Paul McCartney to Mick Jagger, from Barbra Streisand to JLo. The list is nearly endless. At the top of that list sits Quincy Jones, the greatest musical partner of Bruce's life. They were more like brothers, understanding each other on a level deeper than words. And then there was the King of Pop, Michael Jackson, one of history's greatest entertainers, who became our very dear friend.

When Bruce died in 2020, I decided to take the memories and make them into the book you now hold. I wanted to show and tell the story of our life together. I wanted it to feel like you had come over and were sitting with me in my living room, listening to stories and looking through my picture books. Though I miss Bruce every day, it has been a balm to spend time with him in creating this book. We grew up together, we grew old together and we had great fun along the way.

CHAPTER ONE

CHILDHOODS

In the front yard of the bungalow in Impur, Nagaland, India

That's me.

I had the good fortune to be born into an adventurous Swedish-American family. We lived in the foothills of the Himalayas in

Northeast India on the border of Burma in an area known as Nagaland. There, my Swedish father, Bengt Anderson, did missionary work with different Naga tribes, whose forefathers were headhunters. My mother, Edna, whose parents were from Sweden, was a nurse. I was the youngest of five children and was raised by a Naga *ayah* (nanny) whose tribal language I spoke before I spoke English. My father was often away, riding to village churches and schools on the Harley Davidson motorcycle that had been donated by a church in Buffalo, New York.

My parents, Bengt and Edna Anderson,
riding their Harley-Davidson in the Naga Hills

India was then under British rule and we lived a partially British life with tea at four and dressing for dinner—even though it was just the immediate family. In the winters when it was cool we'd go out to the villages on horseback on a trip called a mofussil. We'd travel, a bag of fruit and hardboiled eggs tied to our saddles when traveling in case we got hungry or thirsty, with a whole entourage, all our food, cookware and servants. ('Servants' was the term used in India for any domestic staff.) We would live in tents for days or weeks at a time.

Until we were ready to go to high school we were taught by my mother with books and supplies shipped to us from the States. The curriculum was the Calvert Course out of Baltimore, Maryland. When we were older we left for boarding school. My older siblings Jim,

Audrey and June attended the Mt. Hermon School in Darjeeling, a hill station in West Bengal noted for its famous tea. My brother Bruce and I went to Woodstock School in Mussoorie, a hill station north of Delhi in the foothills of the Himalayas. Though it seemed normal at the time, it was a wildly different upbringing from just about everyone else I'd ever meet.

My 5th birthday party. The Naga children's clothes were donated by the mission.

Brother Bruce and I watching a tribal dance performed for the British Governer of Assam

Traveling on horseback was our main form of transportation

Naga missionary Kijung Ao, with a Naga headhunter who is wearing a necklace of brass faces, one for every head he took

When my older siblings were away at boarding school I was left to my own devices. Our Naga *dhobi* (the man who did our laundry) had a daughter my age named Alice and we became fast friends. My father built a playhouse for us kids on the hill behind the bungalow, and we played with dolls given to us by the White Cross Missions in America. Alice was from the Ao tribe and her village was Mopungchukit. My family would go on furlough back to the States every seven years and I would bring some toys back to the Naga jungle. Imagine Alice and I playing with my new Judy Garland and Lana Turner paper dolls!

When the other kids were home from school we would make our own fun in the jungle. Once when my brothers were chucking spears at banana trees, imagining them to be predators, my leg got in the way and a spear sliced right into it. Somehow it healed without stitches. I still have the scar that shocked my friends and family.

June, Audrey, Jim and I on a bamboo raft at "Dikku Pani,"
a tributary of the Brahmaputra River

Once, my family was riding on horseback through rice paddies on the side of the hills to get to the river Dikupani. After making camp, the servants cut some bamboo and made us the perfect raft for floating down the river. That night, as we slept in our tents, we heard a tiger prowling outside, making a predatory coughing sound. One of the servants grabbed my dad's gun and shot into the air. They made fires and kept them burning all night to keep the tiger at bay. But when we awoke the next morning, we found claw marks on the tent we'd been sleeping in. We were lucky the tiger didn't kill us or the horses!

The cuisine at home in the Naga Hills was based on what was available. We had a *khansama* (cook) named Shilo who only spoke Assamese, which we all had learned. I spoke Ao Naga before I spoke

English because my *ayah*, Tsunkumla, was from the Ao tribe. We raised chickens and sheep, and occasionally someone from the village would bring us the leg of a cow they had butchered. There was no electricity, hence no refrigeration, so we ate what we could and anything leftover was cooked and canned by my mother and Shiloh. We had a beautiful garden just below the bungalow with fruit trees: pears, bananas, guavas, lemon, limes, oranges. Vegetables in the garden included potatoes, onions, carrots and tomatoes. Our *mali* (gardener) took care of the garden and Naga school boys would cut the lawn with sharp *daos* (long knives that once were used for head hunting), singing as they went.

All cleaned up for teatime, with our ayah *(nanny) Tsungkumla*

We had tea on the verandah every afternoon. This was, of course, Assamese tea with milk and sugar, served with tinned sardines on toast, along with cookies and cakes baked by my mother in our kerosene oven. When she couldn't get yeast, she would send the servants to the village to bring back rice beer, which she turned into a starter for the bread.

Meals were served on mother's fine china, which had been purchased in Calcutta. Dinner was at eight, served in the dining room by candlelight. Faces and hands were scrubbed, hair was neatly combed, and we were on our best behavior. The fare was everything from soup to nuts, every night—not exactly what you would imagine for a missionary family deep in the jungle. The British influence traveled far. It was even fancier when we had guests. That's when we would dress for dinner. The D. C. (District Commissioner) and his entourage would come to visit and we would serve high tea. During the war it could be American military personnel on their way to Burma and China or people from the American Mission. Life could be lonely out there and guests were more than welcome.

All this might give the impression that we were living high on the hog, so to speak. But that wasn't at all the case. We lived on donations from churches and individuals in the States as well as a stipend from the mission society. But back then an American dollar went far.

• • •

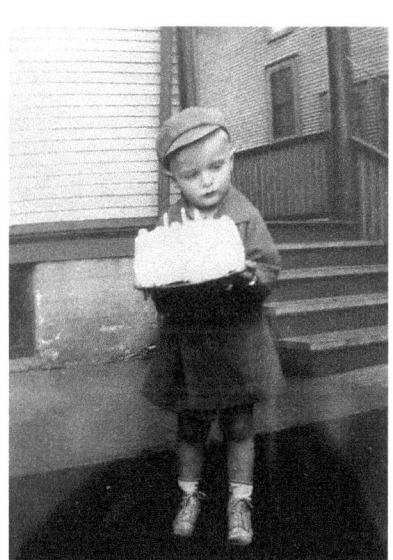

Young Bruce carrying his birthday cake, Minneapolis, Minnesota

That's Bruce.

I knew him from the time I was in the womb. Every seven years, my parents returned from India to America, and my father preached at various Baptist churches to raise money for the missions. Not long before I was born, they took such a trip. One day, at a church in Cokato,

Minnesota, Ellsworth and Louise Swedien were in attendance with their newborn son Bruce, as were my father and pregnant mother. Bruce yelled the whole time. Later in life, he used to joke that he was yelling to me, "Come out now! I want to meet you!"

Cowboy!

Bruce and I might have come from different planets.

He was the only child of musician parents. His father, whose parents had come to the States from Sweden, was an organist, pianist, composer, choir director, electronic designer and teacher. His mother, from a French Canadian father and an English mother, was a soprano, pianist and composer. A lot of their musical activities were in the massive First Baptist Church in Minneapolis. Bruce had plenty of studies in music: piano, voice, drums. One summer Bruce helped his dad tune the pipes of the church's big pipe organ!

Bruce and his mother, soprano Louise Swedien

But it was capturing sounds that captured his attention. When he was eleven his parents gave him a disc recorder and ten minutes later he knew what he was going to do for the rest of his life. He had a little studio in the basement and a ham radio station in the garage so he could broadcast his recordings to the neighborhood.

Recording anyone and everyone was how he learned his craft, soon graduating to a more professional tape recorder. He learned about acoustics and great music from going with his mother to Minneapolis Orchestra rehearsals where she sang in the Women's Chorus. The music was Mahler and the conductor was the famed Dmitri Mitropolous. These early experiences provided a strong foundation for his future. Later in his life he said, "There's a little bit of my mom and dad in everything I've done."

Bruce's musician parents, Ellsworth and Louise Swedien

Ellsworth playing a synthesizer

Bruce (right) sang bass in the school vocal quartet "The King's Messengers"

We were just little kids during the Second World War, but it had an unforgettable impact on us. In Minneapolis, Bruce and his fellow students had to do 'duck and cover' drills in school, families were glued to their radios, stories of Morse code and fighter planes were everywhere. An awareness of "the enemy" was ever-present. Tragic news about lives lost, some of them family or friends. There were blackouts, rationing, air raids even in Minnesota. Bruce had a family member who was only six when they were looking for Hitler—she searched all over her front porch. At the start of the war, Honeywell hired Bruce's dad to work on the Norden bombsight for the US Armed Forces. It was a tachometric design that gave precision measurements of an aircraft's ground and speed direction. His dad's electronic skill and prowess were evident again when, in 1949, he and John Goodell designed the Mastersonic Organ: a seven-octave electronic organ designed to produce pipe organ sounds. It was a huge, complex and expensive machine. They are even cited in the Oxford Dictionary of Music. You can see where Bruce got his electronic wizardry from!

• • •

My family was out of touch at the beginning of the war because it took a week for news to come to us from Calcutta via the only English newspaper available, *The Statesman*. Japanese troops were assembling on the border of the Assam Province, where Nagaland was situated. Telegrams went back and forth to the American Consulate. We finally left India in 1942, sailing out of Bombay on the USS Wakefield, a former luxury liner turned troop ship. My father had to sign us into the U. S. Navy. We sailed to Madagascar, then to Cape Town, South Africa, across the Atlantic and up the east coast of South America, all the while zig-zagging to avoid being torpedoed by German submarines. Two days out of New York, several of the male passengers, including my dad and brother Jim, were held at gunpoint (we were never told why) when we were being pursued by a German sub. A US destroyer escort came to the rescue and we made it into the harbor of the Brooklyn Navy Yard under the watchful eye of the Statue of Liberty. We lived the next two years in St. Paul, Minnesota. My days were spent in an American school where I felt like a foreigner. I remained a Naga to my bones through it all and was happy when we were finally given clearance to return to India and back to Nagaland in 1944. When we arrived in Kohima we were shocked to see the destruction all around. The Japanese troops had advanced into India through Nagaland, where they were stopped in a famous battle. British and Indian forces won but over 4,000 soldiers died. The British District Commissioner's compound was completely destroyed, as was much of the city and surrounding area. Our bungalow had thankfully sustained only minor damage.

India gained independence from Britain in August of 1947 and was divided into India and Pakistan. Fifteen million Hindus, Muslims and Sikhs fled from their homes to get to their 'side' of the new borders. It was total chaos. In March of 1948 my brother Bruce and I were going to take the long train journey to Woodstock School, a co-ed boarding school situated in the foothills of the Himalayas—over fifteen hundred miles of travel. I was fourteen, he was sixteen. Independent travel was not unusual for missionary kids back then. Taking the train from

Mariani, we headed for Calcutta, along with all our supplies for the nine months we would be away at school. This was my first trip away from home without our parents, but I was brave and strong from growing up in the Naga Hills and I had my very capable brother Bruce by my side. After crossing the territory then known as East Pakistan, guards had us get down from the train and searched our luggage. Hundreds of Hindu refugees were climbing onto the moving train; some tied themselves to the train, while others climbed onto the roof, which became a solid mass of humanity.

At one point, the train stopped for several hours. When Bruce and I went to investigate, we saw a large crowd of people standing by the engine. Pushing our way through the crowd, we could see that the engine had hit and killed a cow. No one would touch the cow, thus admitting that they were Muslim, as the train at that time was still in India. There was nothing else to do except for Bruce and me to drag the poor beast off the tracks so that the train could continue on its way.

In Calcutta, we were joined by more students on their way to Woodstock. All of us were in total shock by what we had just experienced but desperately relieved to see each other and to be on our way out of there. None of us would ever forget the horrible sights of that bedlam.

· · ·

Woodstock School in the foothills of the Himalayas

Woodstock School was founded in 1854 and is situated at 7,500 feet in the foothills of the Himalayas. It was recently featured in an Architectural Digest article showcasing the world's nine most beautiful boarding schools. Author Pearl Buck visited in 1962 and wrote: "*It may be a good thing to live on the top of mountains and on the edge of precipices—you learn early not to fear the heights and depths.*"

Woodstock had an American curriculum designed to prepare students for universities in the States. At that time the students were mostly American and British, sons and daughters of various foreigners living in India. My brother Bruce was well-loved by all at Woodstock; they called him 'Andy.' He acted in plays, excelled in sports and academics and was very much his own person. I tagged along—rode on his coattails, so to speak. But I made many friends and had good times sneaking out of the dorm, crashing British Army officer dances. There was a *mochiwala* (cobbler) in the bazaar who would make exact replicas of saddle shoes for us from pictures in American catalogs. We were always hungry and always sneaking food. We wore socks on our hands at night in the cold weather. To this day, I am still good friends with my roommate, Mary Chacko Russell. Our daughter Roberta went to India in 1991 to teach in the Woodstock music department. She taught piano and voice, directed the choir and headed the Music Department. The choir even performed movements of the Mozart Requiem—not an easy task at over seven thousand feet where the oxygen was a bit thin. She remembers her year at Woodstock as one of the best ever, is still in touch with many of her students and colleagues there, and ended up living in India for over fifteen years. India is like that. It takes hold of you and doesn't let go.

CHAPTER TWO

MINNEAPOLIS

When I was sixteen, my parents decided that it was time for brother Bruce and I to return to the States. He had graduated from Woodstock and was ready to go to college. It only seemed appropriate that I would go back too. So we boarded the Portuguese ship *Canton* in Bombay along with my parents, who would return to India after a fund-raising furlough in America. Bruce and I were to go and live with our brother Jim, along with our oldest sister June and her husband Howard in St. Paul, Minnesota. A big change in our lives was coming.

This time I was excited and eager to get reaccustomed to American life. It was 1950, I was a teenager and America was the place to be. After the chaos of partition and independence, the idea of America seemed serene and peaceful in comparison.

So there I was, a teenage girl on a strict British ship getting ready to cross the Atlantic, more interested in the handsome young officers than checking out the pyramids as we sailed through the Suez Canal. The British passengers looked at us like we were insects because we were wearing jeans, which they had never seen before. They kept asking us, "What is that fabric?" The year was 1950: Jeans were the new fashion and the rhumba was the dance of choice. The ship's band entertained the passengers and dancing was on deck under the stars. Often we would go into the ship's bar to check out the gorgeous cockney bartender, Blackie, though we only drank ginger beer or double espressos. Shipboard romances were brief but memorable, and we gave our sad farewells to these fun-loving guys when we left the ship in Liverpool.

After England we sailed to Gothenburg on a Swedish ship, the *Saga*, and after several weeks of visiting our Swedish relatives we sailed to New York aboard the *Stockholm*. On a later voyage in 1956 this very same ship collided one night with the *Andrea Doria*, a famous Italian luxury liner, off the coast of Nantucket in heavy fog. The *Stockholm* survived, but the *Andrea Doria* sank to the bottom of the Atlantic, killing 51 people and resulting in one of the largest civilian maritime rescues in history.

Once settled in St. Paul, I was sent to the Minnehaha Academy, a private school in Minneapolis. The kids there mocked my Anglo-Indian accent. It was hard to adjust. I felt so out of place, even though I was happy to be back in the States. I was also happy to be back with my siblings—we had been separated for four years. We shared our Indian years and experiences that no one else really understood. To our American relatives and just about everyone else, we were foreigners. Brothers Bruce and Jim were both drafted into the army. Jim was stationed in New Jersey and Bruce was sent to Germany to train dogs for the military. For a while I had a job at the phone company to bring in extra money.

My first brush with show business was when a classmate and I cut school to go and see Dean Martin and Jerry Lewis live at the Radio City Theater in Minneapolis. We were served coffee between the shows and actually got to meet the stars. Very exciting!

One day I was at a Baptist youth picnic in Minneapolis. I really didn't want to hang around with them, so my cousin Beverly and I took a walk through the park instead. Some guys from school happened to drive by in a big blue Plymouth. Bruce Swedien was behind the wheel. A year ahead of me and a big man on campus, he was tall, extremely handsome and had a smooth, low voice. He recognized me from school, stopped the car and said, "Hop in! Let's go get some ice cream." We all drove around for awhile, talking and listening to music on his car radio. When he took me home, he had the music going full blast. It was The Four Aces singing "Tell Me Why" so loudly that my brother-in-law Howard came roaring out of the house shouting, "Turn that thing off!" Bruce and I laughed and exchanged phone numbers. That night he went home and told his parents, "I've met the girl I'm going to spend my life with."

We started dating and often those dates included recording sessions. This was my introduction and initiation into the world of setting up, placing microphones, connecting cables, waiting, repetition and perfection. In spite of our practically opposite backgrounds we hit it off right away. I was so impressed by his talent and skill and we shared a sense of humor, which really clinched it. Our story, which had started in the womb, had now reached another chapter. We were in love. Laughing and loving became our norm, whatever the circumstances, for the rest of our lives.

Here we go!

• • •

Our wedding in Minneapolis. Fae Anderson (brother Bruce's wife)
was my matron of honor and John Day was best man.

We got married in 1953. Not long after our wedding, Bruce got a job as a disc jockey, engineer and salesperson for radio station WMNE in Menomonie, Wisconsin, a little town of about 8,000 people. Bruce loved reading the station ID on the air: "This is WMNE, coming to you from the heart of the Red Cedar Valley." This he did with great vocal style, learned in his ham radio days. The main attraction in Menomonie was a 500 million year-old rock formation called "The Devil's Punchbowl."

So off he went while I, expecting our first child, stayed with his parents in Minneapolis. During his radio show, he frequently dedicated the song "Too Fat Polka (She's Too Fat for Me)," which had a chorus that went, "I don't want her, you can have her, she's too fat for me." Everyone laughed. I was enormously pregnant!

Bruce the DJ in "The Heart of the Red Cedar Valley"

Bruce was on the road selling radio advertising time when our daughter Roberta was born. She was the first grandchild in that generation of Swediens and the first girl in two generations. Bruce's parents were with me when she was born, and they loved her from the first minute. She would grow up to carry on the musical legacy.

WMNE - The first of many control rooms

Now a family of three, we rented a farmhouse outside of Menomonie with a huge barn behind it out in the middle of nowhere. Bruce's duties included going to the station at four in the morning to turn on the transmitter. It was pitch dark out. There I was, alone with the baby. Sometimes there would be a knock at the door, some guy who was lost, or someone who wanted to use the phone. I was absolutely terrified. When Bruce was gone, I would close the door to our basement, which didn't have a lock, and put a chair in front of it. I didn't get much sleep. The headhunters in India seemed safe in comparison. The worst thing they did to us was to tug on our white skin to see if it would come off or pull our hair to see if it was real. That we got used to. They were especially fascinated with the red hair of June and my brothers Jim and Bruce. They wanted to smell it!

I certainly wasn't a traditional housewife. I couldn't cook at all. In India all the food preparation was done by our cook, Shiloh. I was fascinated by it all and spent a lot of time in the cookhouse, watching and tasting. We also received five-gallon tins of Spam, bacon and sauerkraut from a nearby Air Force base. For a while, that was the best meal I could make. Every time Bruce wrapped a project, I'd make him Spam and corn fritters. That became our tradition for the rest of his career.

Bruce's mother really taught me how to cook—especially her famous Swedish meatballs, which were Bruce's favorite. These would later make their way into countless recording sessions in Minneapolis, Chicago and LA as treats for all those hard-working musicians. My sugar cookies were always a hit too. Especially with Quincy and Bruce— the studio foodies.

One day when brother Bruce was still in Germany he passed out. He was sent back to the States, to a military hospital in St. Paul. Tests were done and it was discovered that he had Hodgkin's disease. He had married and had a daughter but tragically died at the age of 22. I was devastated. He was my dear friend and we were a special pair our whole lives, short as his was. We had so many wonderful adventures together. I still miss him.

Brother Bruce and I in the Naga Hills with our dog Keto

• • •

Next we moved to Minneapolis, where Bruce attended the University of Minnesota, majoring in electrical engineering with a minor in music. Schmitt Music Company, the Midwest's top music and instrument dealer, had a recording studio in their building in Minneapolis and they hired Bruce to run it. He was loving that! The work was mostly local bands. It was lean living at first. For our first Christmas together, we bought a tree for 25 cents.

One of Bruce's first breaks came when he recorded Jimmy Dorsey's band. It was Jimmy's final recording. Dorsey was one of the biggest names in the business. He and his brother Tommy were famous both for their music and for introducing the world to a young singer named Frank Sinatra.

I remember Bruce and I looking at each other, excited, knowing something big was coming, and saying, "Here we go!"

Soon the studio business at Schmitt's grew and the store decided to offer the recording facility for sale. Bruce and his dad purchased all the equipment and bought an old 400-seat movie theater on Nicollet Avenue. Originally the Garrick Photoplay Theater, the building was built in 1913 and showed silent movies. Then it was the LaSalle Movie Theater, then it was ours: "Swedien Recording Studios." We worked ourselves dizzy building the studio, leveling the floor, installing all the necessary equipment, and sound-proofing the recording room. Of the studio, Bruce once wrote, "I built those doors. If you look at them you'll see they're very solid, very thick." In order to deaden the sound and save some money, we glued egg cartons to the ceiling and walls. It was all we could afford at the time, but it did the trick. Egg cartons are a high-quality, high frequency acoustical treatment. Cheap and efficient too!

On several occasions while listening to playbacks of songs recorded at Swedien Recording, Bruce noticed a strange chirp when the music stopped. Eventually we discovered that there was a cricket in the echo chamber. The old coal storage bin in the basement of our studio had been cleaned out and the walls plastered and painted to use as an echo chamber. To achieve the desired sound, a speaker was placed in the room and a microphone was placed in the same space to pick up the reverberated sound; this was added to the mix through the control console. Needless to say, the cricket had to be eliminated, so we had the echo chamber fumigated.

I had been taking evening classes in interior design at the University of Minnesota, so I took charge of decorating the studio. Bruce, his dad and I must have done a pretty good job, because Swedien Recording Studios is still in business nearly seventy years later—though today it's known as Creation Audio, owned and run by Steve Wiese. It is still a world-class studio, and our original egg cartons are still there.

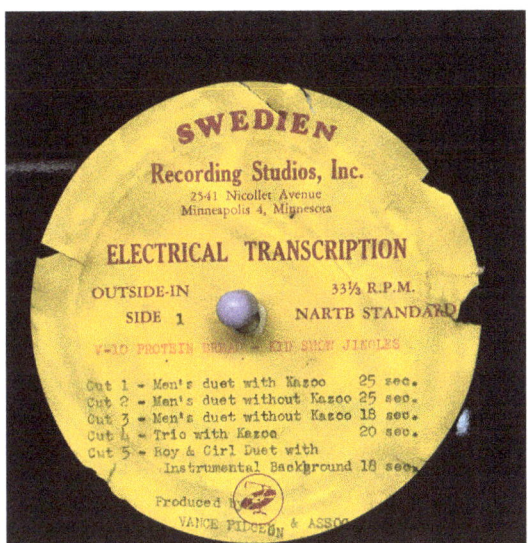

Bruce's early work

Bruce took whatever work he could find, including recording such memorable tracks as "Men's Duet with Kazoo," which was part of the unforgettable album *Protein Bread Kid Show Jingles*. But word got around that there was a new studio in town with a whiz kid at the helm. Geordie Hormel—ironically of the very Spam family from Austen, Minnesota that provided us with so many meals in India—owned a label called Zephyr Records, and he soon began sending his musicians to us.

Jeanne Peterson and Richard Link at Swedien Recording Studios.
Note egg cartons on the ceiling.

Herbie Mann and band (Dave Karr/tenor, Herbie Mann/tenor and flute,
Stu Anderson/bass, Bill Blakkestad/drums, Bobby Timmons/piano)
at Swedien Recording Studios in 1955

Among them was the Herb Pilhofer Octet. The album cover for *Jazz from the North Coast* is a shot of the band playing on a frozen lake, complete with Bruce recording the songs on a cylinder recording machine, with everyone dressed in coats, hats and gloves, and Herb sitting on a ladder holding the score in one hand and a rifle in the other!

Herb Pilhofer's "Jazz from the North Coast"

These were Minnesota jazz guys with a great sense of humor. Bruce also recorded the Bob Davis Quartet. Bob later became the director of music and entertainment for the Playboy Clubs. Other national artists Bruce recorded at Swedien Studios included Art Blakey and the Jazz Messengers, jazz flutist Herbie Mann, The Six Fat Dutchmen polka band and more. Now things were starting to pick up. Geordie ultimately built a phenomenal studio in Los Angeles called The Village Recorder. Years later Bruce recorded with jazz saxophonist Eddie Harris there.

• • •

As Bruce's career grew, so did our family. By 1957, we had three children: Roberta, David and Julie. They inherited a unique life. Our days and nights were turned around. Our house was always full of music coming through big speakers. Their dad didn't work a 9-to-5 job and come home for dinner like the other kids' dads did. In fact, Bruce wasn't there to see any of the kids born until Julie. Anyway, we were all at the studio a lot. Bruce loved to record them talking, singing, whatever. He even recorded our wedding.

Roberta, David and Julie

Maybe most women would have struggled to keep a family and a marriage together under such unique conditions, but I was used to the life of an adventurer. I didn't bat an eyelash. Many studio wives were not happy with the hours and their husbands being gone so much. But it wasn't new to me. My mother held the fort for weeks at a time... sometimes with drunk servants and a tiger on the verandah. My dad was frequently off in the villages—sometimes many miles away, making sure the missionary schools and churches were functioning. The only communication that was available was sending a message by a runner from the village. No electricity, no running water, no neighbors. By comparison I had absolutely nothing to complain about.

We had just purchased our first home, a cute little house on the south side of Minneapolis, for $18,000, when Bill Downs called. He was a famous war correspondent and was covering the United States Air Force "Project Manhigh" for CBS News. It was a series of experiments to test the physiological effects of high altitude flight and was the early testing of astronauts in space. The pilot was in an aluminum capsule about the size of a phone booth, suspended by a helium-filled balloon which took off in Crosby, Minnesota, lifted up to over 100,000 feet before landing in Frederick, South Dakota thirty-two hours later.

Bill needed a sound guy and had heard through the grapevine that the best man for the job was Bruce Swedien. So Bruce went off to chase men in balloons for four days. He had a ball, sleeping on the floors of small airports, with no time to bathe, shave, or call home. These experiments set the stage for the space age and the story made the cover of Life Magazine. Bruce's name started to get around the recording world.

CHAPTER THREE

CHICAGO

There was a guy in Chicago who was changing the art of recorded sound. He owned Universal Recording. Bruce knew about his work and wore out his records. His name was Bill Putnam.

Bill Putnam, founder of Universal Recording

Bruce wrote: "*It was my mom and dad that met him before I did. We were still in Minneapolis. My parents were in Chicago on business, and I told them they had to go see Universal Recording, which at the time was at 111 East Ontario. Of course Bill, being Bill Putnam, was so gracious. He invited them to sit in on the Patti Page session he was doing. Later I got in touch with Bill and he told me that he would soon be looking for a music mixer for Studio B at Universal. By then he knew about my work in Minneapolis. He told me Studio B wasn't ready yet. 'Why don't you come to Chicago now? We'll help you get a job at RCA Victor while we're waiting for studio B to be finished.'"*

It didn't matter that we had just settled in Minneapolis. Bill's offer was a dream come true, so off to Chicago Bruce went while I stayed in Minneapolis with the kids until I could sell the house and move to be with him.

Back then Chicago was one of the major centers of American music, second perhaps only to New York City. Down a ten-block stretch of Michigan Avenue sat all the legendary jazz, R&B, blues, and soul labels such as Chess, Vee-Jay, Okeh, Verve, and Mercury. Chicago was also home to major hubs for RCA, Columbia and other multinational record labels. It was where Bruce belonged.

After selling the house in Minneapolis, the kids and I reunited with Bruce. We rented a house in Wheeling, Illinois, about 45 minutes from the studio. Even in the suburbs you could feel the pulse and energy of the city. We immediately fell in love with Chicago. It was an exciting and sometimes dangerous place.

RCA Studios were located not far from Navy Pier—a massive shipping and recreation facility on the harbor of Lake Michigan that was over three thousand feet long. We would eat delicious smoked fish and shrimp by the bag at Rocky's Bait Shop, a funky little shack by the pier.

In the '50s in Chicago there was a group of gentlemen known as "Da Boiz." These gentlemen—gangsters all—liked to impress their girlfriends, or "molls," who had dreams of music stardom, by hiring Chicago's local musicians to make a record in hopes of a future in the industry. Unfortunately, rarely did this hope materialize. One day Bruce arrived at his new job in RCA Studios to find a moll along with her man and his, shall we say, "security," picking up boxes of her finished record album. Down the elevator the entourage went, then across the street and over the railroad tracks to the lot where their cars were parked. Just as they were about to get in the car, another car came, tires screeching, from the direction of Lake Shore Drive near Navy Pier. The door flew open to a volley of gunshots, leaving the unsuspecting boyfriend crumpled in a puddle of his own blood. Soon after, a local news camera crew appeared on the scene to report on the incident. "Miss Hopeful" took advantage of the situation, and as the cameramen zoomed in on her she held up her newly finished album. Never mind that her boyfriend lay bleeding and almost dead at her feet. This was a free promotion!

Another time, Bruce arrived to set up Studio A for a session when he noticed that the nine-foot Steinway piano was gone. He went out to the receptionist and asked, "Where is the piano?" She said, "Well, the movers came up the freight elevator and said 'We're here to pick up the piano from Studio A.'" Bruce yelled, "What movers?" "Well," she replied, "they had uniforms on that said 'Acme Movers,' and I thought it was okay so I signed their papers. Then they loaded it on the freight elevator and were gone." Acme Movers—it was like a Looney Tunes caper. The piano was never found.

Bruce loved the work at RCA Studios. Along with recording The Dukes of Dixieland, he worked on Chicago Symphony Orchestra albums with Fritz Reiner conducting at Orchestra Hall; a legendary orchestra and a legendary conductor. Bruce was assisting Lewis Layton, the acclaimed classical engineer who had 18 Grammy nominations and 4 wins to his name. He really helped Bruce learn his craft. The CSO has always been one of the top five orchestras in the country, famous for their unparalleled brass section.

Bruce remembered: *"While at RCA, I got to work on some very exciting projects. (Not necessarily always at the RCA Studios on Navy Pier). For instance, I assisted in the recording of The Chicago Symphony Orchestra under the baton of Dr. Fritz Reiner. Actually, when we recorded the CSO it was a bit of a team effort. The man in charge of engineering, and in truth, the guy who really did the recording, was Lewis Layton, a wonderful classical music engineer at RCA Victor. He had a very generous spirit and freely helped me learn my craft. The producer on these sessions was Richard Mohr, another very kind and generous music man.*

We recorded the Chicago Symphony Orchestra in Orchestra Hall on Michigan Avenue. Fritz Reiner was the music director from 1953-1963. He built the CSO into the world-class orchestra that it remains today. I worked at RCA in 1957 and 1958.

Working, watching and learning on those sessions, I remember thinking to myself, "This is why I left Minnesota!"

One recording session—actually a series of sessions—that really stands out in my mind was the Modest Moussorgsky (Maurice Ravel Orchestration) "Pictures at an Exhibition" that we recorded with the CSO in 1957.

I was particularly impressed by the phenomenal trumpet soloist Adolph 'Bud' Herseth. 'Bud' played those trumpet solos on "Pictures" with fantastic skill. The first day we worked on "Pictures," when we took a break, I went out on the stage and talked to Bud. What a great guy. I found out that he was also from Minnesota. A tiny little town called Bertha, Minnesota, as I recall. Not too far from Cokato Minnesota, where my mother was from. What a small world! Instantly I knew that Bud was my kind of guy. He told me of his desire to play his solos "going beyond the notes." Made sense to me. I felt the same way about what I do. I worked with Bud a few times doing sessions at Universal. There were other incredible trumpet players that did most of the studio work in Chicago at that time. Bud's place was with the CSO. Bud [eventually] retired after 53 years as principal trumpet with the Chicago Symphony Orchestra.

I was really fortunate because Dr. Reiner appeared to be quite interested in the recording process. I don't really remember that he truly loved the recording process, but he certainly did appreciate its value. . . . Those incredible recordings that I was involved in in 1957 and 1958 are still considered by many to be among the first truly audiophile recordings.

We would edit the Chicago Orchestra tapes bar by bar, sometimes note by note, until [the music] was as perfect as we thought we could make it. One lasting impression of that period of time for me is that Dr. Reiner made me a part of his innovative new "INCENTIVE" program: "One mistake and you're through." Under Fritz, I learned to edit analog magnetic tape accurately, quickly and above all, musically. I'll never forget him. What fantastic musical and technical experiences! At that time we recorded the CSO on two three-track 1/2 inch Ampex tape machines. One machine recorded the master tape, the other a back-up "safety" master tape. This 20-year-old kid from Minneapolis had never seen anything so high-tech in his life before.

The Chicago Symphony Orchestra under the baton of the great Fritz Reiner

I met and worked with many fantastic musicians that were with the CSO. To name a few that stand out in my memory: Ray Still, principal oboe, Arnold Jacobs, principal tuba, and Dale Clevenger, principal French Horn and recording soloist for the Chicago Symphony

Orchestra (since February 1966). Dale is a well-known Chicago studio musician. I also got to work with Frank Miller, not only with the CSO but in the studio as well. Frank, at that time, was called the greatest living orchestral cellist."

Many of the CSO musicians did free-lance studio work, playing everything from orchestral arrangements to TV and radio commercials (lots of residual dollars there), so we got to know them. Bruce did other classical music projects and at one point was offered a job in Milan, Italy to record opera, but he chose the world of Chicago jazz and big bands instead. Our lives would have been very, very different!

Bruce later wrote: *"My experiences recording for RCA Victor in beautiful, fantastic-sounding Orchestra Hall extended to musical groups other than the CSO. One project that stands out in my memory is recording Dick Schory's New Percussion Ensemble in Orchestra Hall. We recorded an album entitled "Music for Bang Baaroom and Harp!" It was, of course, all percussion.*

This project gave me a real insight into the incredible percussion players working in the Chicago recording scene at that time. We recorded titles like "National Emblem March," "Way Down Yonder in New Orleans," and the memorable "Duel on the Skins." (Hmmm. . .) Many others as well. It was great fun.

The reviews said, "Schory's New Percussion Ensemble is allowed to roam freely in Chicago's Orchestra Hall. This recording captured Schory and his band of lunatics hitting everything but the kitchen sink." The reviewers must have missed something, because I distinctly remember setting up a microphone on a kitchen sink. The critics said the "New Percussion Ensemble" was the "Biggest Battery of Percussion West of Cape Canaveral." It was released in 1959 on the RCA label."

At RCA, Bruce quickly made a name for himself. He understood the science behind the technology. If there was a glitch, he knew how to fix it. But he was more than just a technical genius; he could also read music, and he had great ears. "If someone played a clam," our daughter

Roberta recalls, "he didn't wait for producers to stop the band. He would whistle over the talkback microphone. That would get everyone's attention."

Most days, Bruce would ride the Chicago Northwestern commuter train into the city, a one-hour trip each way, but if a recording session was booked to run late, he would drive his little red Volkswagen Bug. Of course, there were times when a session ran late without warning. As the last train to the suburbs was at midnight, Bruce would call me in the wee small hours of the morning to come into the city to pick him up. Fortunately, we had a terrific babysitter right across the street who was available whenever we needed her.

One late night I was driving to the studio, missed the exit and ended up in a seriously rough neighborhood. I was at a stoplight, not sure which way to turn and a man came towards my car, stepped off the curb and reached to open the passenger door. Thank God I had a new Oldsmobile with electric locks. I got to the studio, trembling, told Bruce and everyone what happened and they all said "Boy, were you lucky!"

• • •

One morning Bill Putnam called Bruce at RCA and said, "Studio B is ready. Want to come work at Universal?" A couple of weeks later he was following Bill around the studios. Bill took him under his wing. It was the opportunity of a lifetime, the best thing that could have happened to Bruce. He would do whatever work came in— commercials, orchestras, voice-overs, jingles—in Studio B during the day and hang out with Bill while he was recording big band dates at night in Studio A. Because Bill was the hottest engineer in the business, all the big bands recorded with him at Universal. It was here that Bruce perfected his art.

"I just about lived with Bill in big, beautiful Studio A, watching and helping wherever I could," Bruce wrote. *"Bill was the father of recording as we know it today. The processes and designs which we take for granted—the design of modern recording desks, the way*

components are laid out and the way they function, console design, cue sends, multitrack switching—they all originated in Bill's imagination. He invented the modern recording console, was the first to use artificial reverberation with echo chambers, more specifically a microphone and speaker in the men's room. He was the first to use tape repeat, the first to use a vocal booth, and one of the first to use 8-track recording. He made several leaps in recording technology that still define the way records are made today." As a kid, Bill also loved electronics; he built a crystal radio with his dad and, like Bruce, had his own ham radio station.

Bruce at the console in Studio B at Universal Recording

So when Bill offered Bruce a job as the engineer of Studio B, Bruce was in seventh heaven. Many nights, Bill and his wife Belinda would take Bruce and me to dinner at Loo Lim's on Rush Street, just under the studio. They were so kind in explaining to me the rugged road ahead: long hours, long absences away from home, and so on.

One of the first major big bands Bruce worked with at Universal was the Woody Herman Band. What a thrill for two kids from Minnesota! Bruce encouraged me to come to the studio to hang out and hear some amazing music. When he was recording Stan Kenton's band, I was at the studio where I met Ann Richards, Kenton's vocalist and also his wife. When she wasn't recording vocals she and I would go shopping at Bonwit Teller on Michigan Avenue. For years I used the great perfume she put me onto, Casaque.

Eventually Bill sold Universal Recording to Bernie Clapper and moved to LA, where he built United Recording on Sunset Boulevard. Frank Sinatra kept him on retainer!

• • •

Mister Kelly's was one of the top nightclubs in America. Glamorous, elegant, and very hip with the country's top jazz musicians and cutting-edge comedians gracing its stage, it was an intimate setting with perfect acoustics and excellent food. The maître d' wore a tuxedo, and charbroiled Chicago steaks and Green Goddess salads were specialties of the house. So were Sarah Vaughan, Dinah Washington, Oscar Peterson, Ramsey Lewis, Lenny Bruce, and Ella Fitzgerald. Evenings there were like concerts, the audience came for the artist. The Chicago Tribune called it "a supernova in the local and national firmament."

And it just so happened that Mister Kelly's was two blocks from Universal Recording. Our lives were forever changed by this proximity.

The London House was the nightclub down on Wacker Drive, owned by the same brothers, George and Oscar Marienthal. Same terrific food, same stellar musicians. Using a reel-to-reel tape machine in the corner of the room, near the stage, Bruce recorded the Oscar Peterson Trio and Sarah Vaughan live at the London House. And he recorded Muddy Waters singing the music of John Lee Hooker live at Mister Kelly's. When we moved to Chicago, we knew we were moving to a big city with great music, but we had no idea that it would be just down the street and that Bruce would be an integral part of forever preserving this ground-breaking music.

It was during a session at Universal in 1959 with Dinah Washington, recording "What a Diff'rence a Day Makes," that Bruce met a young musician who would change our lives forever: Quincy Jones. Quincy, who was only 26 at the time (Bruce was just 25), was already a jack of all musical trades—composer, arranger, conductor, musician, producer. As Quincy later wrote, *"Early in my career I met a young dude at Universal Studio in Chicago by the name of Bruce Swedien, who shared my excitement in creating recorded music images that originated in our own imagination. We have been kindred spirits ever since."*

Dinah was "Queen of the Blues" and I was right there for those sessions in beautiful Studio A at Universal. She walked in wearing an exquisite gray mink coat, went into the vocal booth, took off the coat, threw it on the floor, stood on it in her high heels and sang the whole session, with her male back-up singers behind her, standing on that mink! As Quincy said about her, *"She could take the melody in her hand, hold it like an egg, crack it open, fry it, let it sizzle, reconstruct it, put the egg back in the refrigerator and you would've understood every single syllable."* The title song of that album was a Top Ten hit and would win a Grammy Award for Best R & B Performance.

This was where the Quincy and Bruce duo started. It was pure kismet, those paths crossing. Later they would together change the history of music.

The next project in 1959 was none other than the Oscar Peterson Trio with Oscar on piano, Ray Brown on bass, and Ed Thigpen on drums. Bruce recorded many albums with that trio in Studio A, including the Songbook Series on Verve Records: *The Gershwin Songbook*, *The Harold Arlen Songbook*, *The Jerome Kern Songbook*, *The Cole Porter Songbook*, *The Duke Ellington Songbook*, and *The Richard Rodgers Songbook*. Later, in July and August of 1961, he recorded the trio's album *The London House Sessions* live. What an experience! Bruce was in seventh heaven. He loved Oscar's playing and would talk about it for the rest of his life. Those projects with the trio would remain some of his favorites of all time.

"To Bruce, The man who <u>knows</u> how to record this trio!
Sincere regards to an Artist!! Oscar Peterson"

I remember sessions with the Count Basie Band and the celebrated jazz singer Joe Williams. It was 1960, the album was *Just the Blues* for Roulette Records, and I was there. Already a veteran at being "one of the gang" in the studio and the control room, I fit in naturally and loved every minute of it. The cacophony of musicians tuning up and practicing riffs, the squeal of tape rewinding, the intense focus and excitement of something exciting about to happen—it was all home to me.

The sessions started at two in the morning when their gig at the club ended and went until dawn. Already very warmed up from the gig, they were ready to put it all on tape. Bruce always said this was an ideal time to work. Friends and fans from the club, called "band flies," would follow the band to the studio. Folding chairs and cases of sparkling burgundy were brought in and the studio was transformed into a party room of happy people. Thank God Studio A was huge!

Joe wanted to revise some of the lyrics so he had me writing down all his changes. What a great guy, as were most of the jazz players at that time. These musicians were really nice people. Polite, fun, professional. A lot of characters, but no divas or troublemakers. The party and tuning up would carry on and then suddenly everyone sat down and you could hear a pin drop. Over the talkback mic Bruce would say, "Trav'lin' Light, take one." Basie, conducting from the piano, would give the upbeat, the band would come in and it was perfection. Track after track was laid down and voilá, they had created an entire album. It would end at four, five or even six the next morning.

After these sessions, I would help Bruce put the studio back to normal, putting the chairs away, coiling cables, etc. to get everything ready for the morning jingle session. (Back then, engineers didn't have assistants.) We'd drive the long drive back home to a sleepy babysitter, go to bed at last and it would all start again the next day.

• • •

Bruce recorded several albums with Keely Smith and Louis Prima with the band known as Sam Butera and the Witnesses. Great musicians and great fun! One night after the session we all went to the "Chez Paree," a fantastic nightclub complete with a comedian, scantily dressed dancers, and a singer. Keely's deadpan expressions were unforgettable– she was quite a character. Fabulous music, and what a great voice.

On one occasion Bruce was working on an album project with the Smothers Brothers, the famous comedy team. When I walked into the control room they let loose with wolf whistles. I smiled and said, "Thank you." They smiled and said, "That was for Bruce."

When Bruce was recording Mimi Hines she decided the vocal booth was too warm so she removed her blouse. The band loved it. Mimi and her husband Phil Ford were a comedy team, plus she had quite a career as a pop singer.

The amazing Sarah Vaughan's album *You're Mine You* was a project that had Bruce and Quincy working together again. Twenty-seven years later they would again be recording her on Quincy's Grammy-winning album *Back on the Block*. Bruce also recorded her on her album *Sweet and Sassy*, with Lalo Schifrin arranging and conducting. Bruce loved recording the huge orchestra that you hear behind her gorgeous voice. Those sessions were unforgettable.

Bruce remembers Duke Ellington this way: "*I can close my eyes and see him walking into the studio. He had a very regal bearing. I mean, the way he carried himself was like he was a member of royalty. When Duke walked into the studio, you instantly felt something important was about to happen. And it always did.*"

He also had vivid recollections of their work together in Studio A: "*I remember Duke sitting at the piano during a take with a very thoughtful expression on his face. All of a sudden he got up from the piano and tore off a little 4 x 6 inch piece of music manuscript paper. Next he scribbled a little four-bar riff on this scrap of music paper and quietly tippy-toed around the studio showing this fragment of music paper first to the saxes—they would all nod—then over to the trumpet section and then the trombones. This was all while the tape was rolling! At the appropriate musical moment, Duke would stand in the middle of the band, raise his arms and with a great sweeping motion, conduct this little gem and it would become part of the arrangement. Duke Ellington loved music, he lived music and I don't think I have been the same since I met him. Working with him made me realize how much music, and the recording of music, really meant to me.*"

In 1962 Bruce recorded Frankie Valli and the Four Seasons' single "Big Girls Don't Cry." It hit #1 on the Billboard Hot 100. Frankie and the band received the Grammy nomination for the Best New Artist of 1962, and "Big Girls Don't Cry" was nominated for Best Rock and Roll Recording as well as being inducted into the Grammy Hall of Fame in 2015.

He also recorded the St. Olaf Choir that year. Bruce loved recording choirs. That was the case from his early days as a kid with his disc recorder in Minneapolis throughout his entire career... including the Andraé Crouch choir on many of the Quincy and Michael projects. Another choir he recorded in Chicago was the Beautiful Zion Choir. He did many albums over the years with pianist and composer Kurt Kaiser on Word Records.

This workload at Universal was serious. On many occasions Bruce would be at the studio by 9 AM, only to drive home about noon the next day, shower, change clothes, eat and drive back to the studio for the next gig. Many nights he didn't get any sleep. But he loved his work, and who could blame him? He often said "I am one lucky dude!" The family went with the flow. Having lived like this for already a decade, we were used to it. I never complained about him not being home enough. We were a team and this was our life. It was often unpredictable and sometimes thrilling. And it would only get more so.

• • •

Around this time we purchased a sweet little red brick house in Mt. Prospect, a suburb on the northwest side of Chicago. It was our first home. Three bedrooms and central air conditioning! This was the life. It was here that we started our Great Dane habit—a habit that has lasted more than 50 years. Our first Dane, Gus, was a Harlequin, white with black splotches. He was very white with blue eyes and a black spot over one eye. Seeing a photo of Gus at a session, an ad agency guy thought he would be perfect for an ad for Tareyton cigarettes, whose motto was "I'd rather fight than switch." But it never came to be. Gentle Giants are what Danes are called and he fit the bill.

Happy in the kitchen with Gus the Great Dane puppy

Another habit that was started in this house was Siamese cats. Bruce always said he couldn't stand cats. But I had to have a little feline around the house. My parents had finally moved back to the States from India and were living in Wyoming—a bit like the back ways of India, if you squint. They were as happy as can be expected there. Of course they had animals around and one of their Siamese cats had just had a litter of kittens. They were coming to the midwest for a visit and I asked them to please bring a kitten for us. All of this was planned without Bruce knowing a thing. It was going to be a surprise. I was prepared for anything except for what happened. Bruce fell in love with her! He was a cat man for the rest of his life. We named her Kristina. She had a very kinked tail, which was a sign of good luck. A few years later she was bred with composer/arranger Mike Simpson's beautiful Siamese male, TickTock. Their romance took place in our house and it served as a lesson in the birds and the bees for our kids. Or at least we thought so.

Another habit that really developed around this time and would continue for decades was boating. Hard to imagine we'd have any time but we made it happen. Our first boat was a little aluminum outboard back in Minneapolis that we'd haul to this lake or that. Bruce had been on boats as a kid and loved getting out on the water, revving up the engine and zooming off towards the horizon. The sea, large or small, was his passion. There was always a book about underwater life by Jacques Cousteau in his briefcase. He would read on the train to and from the city and come home and share the colorful stories with the family.

Now that we were close to the mighty Lake Michigan, our boating got more serious. All of our boats were called *Odin* after the #1 Viking god. Vacations were fun, family and friends came aboard… and the cats and the dog were always members of the crew. Oh, and we had a great sound system on the boat too.

Sometimes Bruce's parents would drive down from Minneapolis for holidays, or we would pack the kids and the animals in the car and drive eight hours back to our old stomping grounds to see family and old friends. As good as it was to rest and relax a bit, going back home to Chicago and its music scene was always exhilarating. "What's the next project?" was always the buzzing question in our lives.

The famous song "Moon River" was composed by Henry Mancini and Johnny Mercer for the movie *Breakfast at Tiffany's*. Bruce recorded Jerry Butler singing it. Jerry helped lay the foundation of the soul movement in the 50's, collaborating with icons such as Ray Charles, Otis Redding, Curtis Mayfield, and Sam Cooke. He was called "The Ice Man" because of his smooth, cool as ice baritone voice, and he was the very first artist to record "Moon River." The session was booked for 8 AM. Crazy! This was because Jerry was appearing at a club in Philadelphia and had to take the red-eye to Chicago to record at Universal and get back to Philly after the session. That was how important the sound was at Universal and Bruce was a big part of that. He had to get to the studio at 7 AM to set up and make coffee. Musicians came in around 7:45. Riley Hampton was the arranger. Bruce remembers that "Riley gave the downbeat, we made three or four takes and the rest is history."

• • •

One Saturday afternoon, the wives of the musicians all gathered in our living room for a surprise baby shower for Jamie Silvia, the beautiful and talented first-call Chicago studio singer. It was not your average gathering. They were the wives of trumpet players, drummers, back-up singers, arrangers, conductors, engineers, sax, flute, guitar, piano, bass guys. The talk was about studios, club gigs, obnoxious ad agency guys, crazy hours, musician gossip, and trading strategies on how to raise a family in this weird world of music recording.

On another occasion I almost lost my happy home. Bruce had set out two of his mics by the front door because he was planning on taking them to the studio. Thinking he was getting rid of them I got excited about turning them into lamp bases for our recreation room. "No way!" he yelled. "Those are my RCA 44 BX mics!" So much for cute lamps.

Microphones and recording gear were Bruce's world and a big part of ours too; in fact, we have most of our family holidays on tape. Bruce would sling his Nagra portable reel-to-reel tape machine over his shoulder and walk around the house with a microphone interviewing everyone in his best radio voice. Of course every tape would start with something like, "Today is December 24th, it's 4 o'clock, and we are here in the kitchen with the cooks. And what is your name? How old are you? What did you get for Christmas?" This went on every year. Every person had their holiday interview, from the little kids to the most senior great-aunt. Or maybe on a Saturday afternoon he'd fire up his microphone and just talk to the kids and record it. And maybe the dog would sing! It's all on tape.

Speaking of microphones... Bruce started his now-famous collection of microphones in Minneapolis. As the years went by, the collection grew and he started using only his mics to record with, hauling them to the studio. (By the time we got to LA, he had huge, bright yellow Anvil cases for the mics and would have a guy named "Catfish" transport them to whatever studio he was working on at the time.) It's a legendary collection, unlike any other.

Speakers were a part of everyday life too. Even in our little home in Mt. Prospect, Bruce had audio in every room (even the bathroom), each equipped with its own little speaker and volume knob. Music was piped into these speakers from the basement. It could be anything from the Oscar Peterson Trio to the Grand Canyon Suite to a Stan Freberg comedy album. Where most wives would have some armchairs and a side table in the living room, we had a gigantic speaker. It was beautiful blonde wood, so that helped. And when the neighborhood had their annual summer block party, guess who was in charge of sound? And boy, did he deliver!

Of course the neighbors were used to music coming from our house on the corner. Trumpets, drums, vocals, big bands, full string sections, you name it—it all wafted out of our windows into the neighborhood. Sometimes pretty cranked up. It was definitely not the music you'd expect from a little red brick house in a Catholic suburb.

Hugh Hefner, famous for his Playboy empire, wanted to make an album with Chicago jazz singer Johnny Janis. Don Costa did the gorgeous orchestra arrangements, Dick Marx conducted, and Bruce engineered. Bruce would come home and play the tracks, mostly slow torch songs with Johnny's incredibly emotional vocals. The whole family would be sitting at dinner raptly listening to this incredible music, kids included. Years later Bruce would listen to the record and call Johnny up, just to tell him how much he loved that album.

The next year Bruce recorded the great Ramsey Lewis' (of "In Crowd" fame) album *Wade in the Water*, which hit #2 on the Billboard Top Soul Album charts and won a Grammy for Best Rhythm and Blues Group Performance. They had recorded the album *Never on Sunday* a few years earlier. Two players from Ramsey's trio would get a new piano player and formed Young-Holt Unlimited, who Bruce did a lot of work with for Brunswick Records. The very famous "Soulful Strut," with that distinctive trumpet opening, was one of their big hits. That record was played at home a lot.

The musicians in Chicago were all five-star. It was a friendly group of incredible players, singers, composers, and arrangers, all of whom could cross over into any style without blinking an eye: jazz, pop, classical, jingles, rock, country, folk, you name it. They could sight-read any chart you put in front of them and record it on the spot. Time is money in this biz and when the studio meter is running there isn't time for clams.

Dick Marx was one of Chicago's premier jazz pianists. He was also a composer, arranger, and conductor. He and the equally talented jazz bass player and violinist Johnny Frigo had the house band at Mister Kelly's, playing every Monday and Tuesday night. Pianist Marty Rubenstein also had this gig. Bruce worked with these guys almost every day at Universal on albums and jingles. Dick was married to Ruth Marx, a jingle singer and they became great friends of ours for many years. Their son Richard would go on to be a big pop music star, with his hit song "Right Here Waiting" selling over 30 million copies. Our daughter Roberta used to babysit Richard. He was a handful back then. But once he was asleep, she'd go and practice on Dick's beautiful Steinway B.

• • •

During the day the studios were always booked solid with jingle sessions. Jingles are the music for radio and TV commercials and were often nifty little tunes that would get stuck in your head. I guess that was the idea. They were composed by some of Chicago's best musicians, among them Dick Marx. Dick composed, arranged, and conducted the music for United Airlines, Kellogg's, Pop Tarts, Hamm's Beer, Chicken of the Sea Tuna, Marlboro, Dial Soap, and the well-known 'Fly the Friendly Skies of United.' The jingles were often sung by members of The J's with Jamie, a vocal quartet featuring singer Jamie Silvia. Singers from The Hi-Lo's, with arrangements by Gene Puerling, were also on a lot of sessions, jingles and otherwise.

For all of our Chicago years we were friends with many of these people and their spouses. We had dinners, outings, sometimes even vacations together. The recording scene is unique and it was nice to have friends who knew what you were talking about.

While still at Universal Recording in Chicago, Bruce met and worked with the jazz drummer Fred Wacker and his wife Jana. Jana was a gorgeous Italian-American singer from New Jersey and Fred was a member of the Wacker family, as in "Wacker Drive." Their albums included all the fantastic studio musicians who lived in the city, such as Johnny Frigo on string bass, Dick Marx on keyboards, Frank Rullo on drums, Earl Backus on guitar and percussion, and Kenny Soderblom on sax, flute, and clarinet.

Fred and Jana had a beautiful home in Lake Bluff on the North Shore of Chicago. On many occasions we were invited to parties at their home. Often at their Christmas parties they would include the society set, along with their musician friends. At one Christmas party they had hired a bartender who was also a comic. He would pretend to be drunk and crawl on his knees under the beautiful grand piano while holding a tray of drinks. Hilarious! It was especially thrilling to meet Jim Kimberly (of Kimberly-Clark) as we had often admired his gorgeous yacht "The Silverfox," which was docked at Belmont Harbor in Chicago.

The Swedien family in Chicago

The kids loved the fact that they could tell their friends they knew the Jolly Green Giant of "Ho-Ho-Ho! Green Giant" fame. That was Len Dresslar, one of the Chicago jingle singers and the bass voice of the group The Singers Unlimited. Bruce came home one day and told us about patching in the voice of Thurl Ravenscroft from San Diego to Chicago to create a soon-to-be-famous commercial for Kellogg's Frosted Flakes. Thurl was the voice of Tony the Tiger's *"They're Grrrreat!!"*

But it was the ad agency guys that made the world of jingles special. Often wandering into the control room after a three-martini lunch they were ready to be artistic. Bruce came home with amusing stories. Once one of these agency guys was sitting in the control room with Bruce and over the talkback mic said to the drummer, "Hey, ya know, it's missing something. Could you just put a little more magic in the drums?" They did another take and the drummer stopped, stood up and hollered

"Abra-the-fucking-cadabra!" Another time one of these agency guys decided to tell Bruce where the microphones should go. Bruce looked at the guy and said, "You know, that's a great idea," then whispered something to his assistant, who proceeded to go into the studio and move the mics every which way before putting them back exactly where they were in the first place. They did another take and the guy said, "Oh man, yeah! That's what I was talking about!"

• • •

Bruce pioneered stereo recording. *"I have always felt that we can reproduce the sound of music, plus the feeling of music, more emotionally by using good stereo recording technique,"* he once wrote, *talking about the early days of the technology. "But at that point in time, the people that ran the record companies didn't think there was much of a future in stereo. I remember one guy—I won't name him, he was a big executive with a major label. He said that, to him, 'stereo is like taking a shower with two shower heads. . . and you wouldn't take a shower with two shower heads, would you?' Shows you what small thinkers they were. They had so little trust in the future of stereo that they wouldn't even pay for the tape or the extra stereo tape machine to record those priceless musical performances in stereo. So I did it on my own. (A few other engineers at that time did the same thing.) We built a separate control room just for stereo. And we had to disguise it. We set up the separate control room for the stereo in the back part of the studio complex, so that the record moguls wouldn't see the stereo machines and think they were paying for extra tape, or machines, and go crazy on us. Even with this bold guerrilla effort on the part of a few, think of all the beautiful stereo recordings that vanished into thin air, because of small thinking on the part of the narrow-minded people that held the purse strings of the business."*

• • •

David in the studio

Bruce also loved to take the kids to the studio and explain everything to them. Our son David was fascinated by all the equipment and was very curious about the process, but it was Roberta who felt most comfortable in the studio. Universal was like a second home to her. One Saturday Bruce was recording Tommy Sands, who was married to Nancy Sinatra, Frank's daughter.

"While my dad and I were waiting for the musicians to arrive, I sat down at the piano and started playing a piece by Sibelius, when suddenly I felt a pair of hands on my shoulders," Roberta remembers. "It was Tommy Sands. He smiled and said some encouraging words to me about my classical music pursuits. What a nice man!"

While Tommy recorded, Roberta and Nancy hung out in the control room. Another time, Bruce was doing a beer commercial with the group Cream—Eric Clapton, Ginger Baker, and Jack Bruce—and all three of our kids accompanied their dad to the studio to meet these rock 'n' roll heroes and watch them work. Never once did any of these major artists complain about us hanging out in the studio. We never gave them reason to.

While Bruce showed our kids the creative life, I tried to pass on some of my gustiness. Roberta took an early interest in music and soon was accepted into the Chicago Conservatory of Music. I'd make the hour-long drive from the suburbs into the city, drop her off on Van Buren and Michigan, give her money for a taxi, and tell her, "Never forget to tip the driver!" At twelve years old, she learned to be independent, just like her mother. After her lesson, she'd tell the cab driver to take her to Universal, where she would sit in the control room with Bruce and watch the session. Sometimes she'd go into Studio B to practice. She has since become a globe-trotting performer and music teacher.

"At one session, I was sitting in the control room next to one of the singers," Roberta recalls. "She opened her very expensive baby blue calfskin clutch purse to get a cigarette, nudged me with her elbow, pointed to a small pearl-handled revolver nestled there in her purse and raised her eyebrows as if to say, 'Honey, you gotta be ready for *anything*.'"

• • •

Both of our families have always had a strong Swedish identity. This included the food. We would shop for Swedish groceries at Oscar Schott's in Chicago's Swede Town: fresh lingonberries, pickled herring, Swedish cheese, and horseradish. We even had *lutfisk* at Christmas: dried codfish that had been soaked in lye and was boiled and served with potatoes and cream sauce—an acquired taste to be sure, but we actually liked it. Bruce would put on LPs of Christmas music from Sweden, in Swedish, which the kids learned to sing. Our houses and boats were full of Swedish decor, from the famous wooden orange horses (*Dalahäst*) from Dalarna, where Bruce's grandmother was from, to elegant *Orrefors* crystal, to pale Swedish linens on the table. Our business logo was, and still is, a Viking ship, our studios were called West Viking Studios, and, as I mentioned previously, all of our boats were called *Odin*. No question about where our blood was from!

Our Viking ship logo

For several years Bruce had been mentioning that he'd love to play guitar. He often talked about Goya, a Swedish-made guitar. One day while I was visiting Universal Studio I mentioned this to one of the engineers who was also a musician. He said the Chicago Guitar Gallery was probably the best place to find a Goya, so we made plans to meet there one Saturday afternoon. I hopped on a train and with cash in hand headed for the city. I don't remember the name of this helpful young guy, but what a coincidence—who was there shopping for guitars but Peter, Paul, and Mary. They were in town to play a gig. They noticed that we were novices and soon they helped me choose the correct instrument. Bruce was thrilled. He loved to play an old Swedish hymn on it from time to time, but then it stayed in its case. I decided that I might like to study guitar, so I signed up for lessons at a local music school owned by Art Van Damme. Art was a well-known jazz accordionist. After about my fourth lesson, Art closed the school and moved to LA. I knew I was bad, but we always joked about just how bad I was that he left town!

In costume to sell Swedish candles

I had a short-lived job as a Swedish candle promoter. One of our best friends, Sven Arne Rikarp, had a Swedish radio program in Chicago, and near Christmas 1966, he was doing promotion for a Swedish candle company. He had this silly idea to have me dress in a Swedish folk costume and display these candles. Mostly I worked in the malls in the Chicago suburbs. However, one day he had me drive all the way to Gary, Indiana. Not many Swedes there, although in one of life's strange coincidences, there was a young boy named Michael who was starting to make a name for himself, singing with his four brothers.

• • •

Ken Nordine, "The Voice of God,"
on the air with their radio show "Now Nordine"

Around this time, Bruce built a studio for the talented voiceover artist, jazz poet, Word Jazz creator, and fellow Swede Ken Nordine. The studio was on the third story of the Nordine home, a 120-year old mansion on Kenmore Avenue. Today, Ken is best known for his cult classic album *Colors*. Bruce recorded Ken and they put together a very hip, creative, avant-garde, sometimes silly, sometimes philosophical and poetic radio show called *Now Nordine*. An example of Ken's poetic imagination is his poem "Seven Ways of the Meek," where he changed the names of the days of the week to Dumbday, Bluesday, Endday, Blurday, Cryday, Shatterday, and Stunday. Bruce often said Ken's voice sounded like God's voice, or maybe what God wished his voice sounded like.

Ken was a big deal at the Swedish Club of Chicago. We were often invited to their incredible Swedish Christmas dinner, known to Swedes as *Julbord* or Christmas Table. It was grand beyond belief, complete with a roasted boar at one end of the banquet table, with an apple in its mouth and a huge, elegant ice sculpture of a swan in the middle.

One time when we were cruising on our boat on Lake Michigan we made a stop in Escanaba, Michigan. The Nordines had a summer home nearby in Spread Eagle, Wisconsin. While we were there they took us to dinner at the country club—great friends, great food. Gentlemen were required to wear a jacket at dinner and Bruce had forgotten his, so Ken loaned him a cool black leather blazer. When we got to the club, Ken, often the prankster, proudly and loudly introduced him as the esteemed Dr. Swedien, world-famous gynecologist. Several of the local ladies gathered around and peppered him with their intimate medical questions. Bruce's eyes popped and his face went twenty shades of red.

• • •

In 1966, Dick and Ruth Marx encouraged us to move to Highland Park, where they were living. It was a beautiful town on the North Shore of Lake Michigan and the site of the Ravinia Festival, which was the summer home to the Chicago Symphony Orchestra.

We made the move, and I soon found a classic white brick house with black shutters on a curving tree-lined street. It was a definite step up from Mt. Prospect. But the house was a big, old fixer-upper. We tore out cupboards, bathtubs, and dirty carpets. I ripped off the old wallpaper and put up new paper, even on the powder room ceiling. The result was an elegant home worthy of this new neighborhood. The schools were so much better and the kids spent all of their high school years here. I got my first horse, Susie, and boarded her at a nearby stable. I would visit her often and ride on horse trails through the forest preserves. Back in the saddle! It was so nice to have a horse in my life again after all those years in India where our horses were our primary way of travel in the foothills. Susie was just the first of a series of beautiful horses that I had and loved for almost sixty years.

As you may have guessed by now, we were foodies before the term had been coined, and Chicago was the place to be for restaurants. George Diamond's Steakhouse, Gino's Pizza on Rush Street, the

Hapsburg Inn (which started in 1934, the year Bruce and I were born), Hackney's in Glenview—the list goes on and on.

• • •

David onboard the Roamer:
forty-two feet of steel hull

By this time, we had worked our way up from our 15-foot boat through a series of ever larger cabin cruisers. Now, our *Odin* was a steel-hulled 42-foot Chris-Craft Roamer. Bruce was Captain and I was First Mate. We all knew how to coil the lines like pros (not so different from microphone cables), and we all used the nautical language of port, starboard, fore, aft, galley, berth, head; I even took the Power Squadron course in seamanship and navigation. One of Bruce's favorite things to do was to sit in the engine room when we were docked. That was heaven to him: cleaning his twin Chris-Craft 300 horsepower engines, maybe changing a spark plug or two. Bruce loved his equipment!

Our cozy Swedish home vibe (*mysigt*) would extend to the boats as well. The galley and the hold were always well-stocked with provisions. One of our first cabin cruisers didn't have an electric fridge; instead we had a real old-fashioned "ice box." The ice man would cometh in the morning with a huge block of ice held by big metal tongs and carry it below decks. No problem for me after all those years in India! Whenever we came back from our vacations on the boat, tan and rested, we would all be 'rocking'—that wobbly feeling that happens when you're back on dry land and no longer need your 'sea legs.' Even the cats would go staggering down the hall.

In the galley of the boat, Swedish coffee pot on the burner

One summer, we thought it would be fun to make a film about the history of the ports along the eastern coast of Lake Michigan, from Holland to Grand Haven, Luddington, Frankfort, Charlevoix, St. Ignace, and Mackinac Island. We had a lot of fun climbing up lighthouses, interviewing locals, visiting libraries and museums. We learned so much and made many new friends. Early one morning, we pulled out of the harbor at South Manitou Island, a little island we had visited before crossing the lake. The filming was done and we were ready to start for home. Sister Bay, Wisconsin, was our next port of call, fifty miles west. The kids were still asleep in their berths and Bruce and I were up on deck looking at charts and battening down. The skies were gray and we knew we were going to run into some rough seas. We pulled out and before long we were engulfed in black skies and giant twenty-foot rollers. We were in a full gale. It was pea-soup fog, there was no sight of land, and the boat was pitching, straight up and then straight down. Bruce was trying to 'tack'; steering at angles. We were terrified. We all thought we were going to die. Bruce was up on deck yelling, "Mayday! Mayday!" into the ship-to-shore radio, Roberta was up there with him, and I was below decks desperately trying to put a life jacket on Hans, our Great Dane. The other kids were huddled in the forward stateroom. We knew we were lost. Then, miraculously, through the fog, a massive black and white structure suddenly appeared. It was the hull of a giant freighter, hovering high above us, like a massive wall. Bruce got them on the radio and they told us to follow behind in their wake; their mercifully calm, flat wake. Words could never describe the relief we felt. This near-tragedy stayed with all of us for years. I can still see it, feel it, like it was yesterday. If it weren't for the steel hull of that Roamer, we would not have survived.

Back in Chicago, Bruce wrote the script and did the editing of the footage. Our film *North to Mackinaw* was finished, with Ken Nordinc doing the narration and Chicago folk singer Win Stracke doing the music. It played on Chicago TV. No one knew the behind-the-scenes story.

· · ·

In 1969 Bruce got his first Best Engineered Recording, Non-Classical Grammy nomination (he liked to say he was Gramminated) for the album *Moog Groove* by the Electronic Concept Orchestra with Eddie Higgins, produced by Robin McBride for Mercury Records. He and Bruce would later work together in 1970 on the Buddy Miles album *Them Changes*. Back then, the Grammy Awards event was held in five different cities simultaneously: New York, LA, Chicago, Nashville, and

Atlanta. In Chicago that year it was at the Ambassador West Hotel and we were there. Wow, the Grammys! Such an elegant and exciting evening. The Beatles album *Abbey Road* won the engineering award that year. Not bad company!

• • •

Speaking of Bob Moog, here's a behind-the-scenes story Bruce shared with journalist Craig Anderton for the Music Player Network:

Bob Moog flips Bruce Swedien the Bird!" by Bruce Swedien

The following is a true Studio Tale. Some of the dates may be off a bit, but every attempt was made by the author to be accurate. The places and the participants are absolutely precise.

It happened during the summer of 1970 (I think) . . .

I was recording an album at Marty Feldman's great studio in Chicago—Paragon Studios. I was working with the incredible saxophone virtuoso Eddie Harris. Robert Moog was working with us [too]. Bob made some very extraordinary electronic devices for Eddie. Bob and Eddie had done a lot of experimental stuff that never went into production. Bob's favorite was a four-oscillator synthesizer for Eddie. Eddie used it for years and we made several records with it. It was unique. But then, everything that Eddie, Bob and I did for those recordings was unique.

Paragon was a walk-up two story recording studio. You came in at the street and then walked up one flight to the Paragon Recording Studio offices. Then up one more flight of stairs to the studio. And what a studio!

That walk-up was a real pain-in-the-ass. The interesting thing was that after the initial walk-up, people griped and moaned about it, but then after an hour or two working in those great-sounding rooms, with all that great Marty Feldman equipment, there were nothing but smiles and happy faces all around.

Marty Feldman was an excellent small airplane pilot. Recording was Marty's first love but flying small airplanes was a close second love! The console in Marty's studio was a great-sounding desk built by legendary audio design engineer Daniel Flickinger. Marty had designed the control room with all the audio outboard gear installed above the engineers head just like the pilots cockpit in an airplane. It worked quite well as I recall.

We had been working all night on the Eddie Harris album. We had started at 8 PM the night before. I was burned, but that is the way it is sometimes. Besides, the Eddie Harris album was fantastic! That was all that mattered to me.

I was scheduled to start work on a religious record with Dale Evans singing at 10 in the morning. Eddie and his crew and Bob Moog were packing up all their stuff. The musicians and the Religious Record Label Folks arrived at about 10. Dale Evans was there with husband Roy Rogers in tow. (Interesting side note: The label folks had warned me not to ask about Trigger, Roy Rogers' legendary Palomino horse. They said to me that, if Trigger was mentioned in conversation, not to say that he was stuffed. No, he was mounted, I think they told us to say.)

Marty called me on the studio phone and asked me if he could bring them all up into the control room. I said, sure! We were done with Eddie's stuff and they were packing up the gear out in the studio.

So, picture this. In the Paragon control room, myself, seated at the legendary Flickinger, and Marty Feldman behind me, waiting to make sure our clients were all happy. Behind him, three dudes, very restrained, in handsome three-piece suits with ties, from the religious record label. Plus Dale Evans and Roy Rogers waiting for something to happen. . . . The mood in the control room was somber and prayerful. It was a Religious Record Date. It was almost a prayer meeting, but not quite....

All of a sudden, the control room door bashed open and Robert Moog, looking all dignified (the father of the synthesizer), burst in. He ran around to the front of the console directly in front of me, stuck his tongue out and made a very obscene gesture directly at me. (You know the one! With his right hand and his middle finger up! I think it's called Flipping Someone The Bird.)

Everyone in the control room froze in abject horror. You could have heard a pin drop.

Then Robert Moog, the father of the synthesizer, spun on his heel and left without saying a word. Leaving me to explain what had happened.

Of course, behind me, Marty Feldman was absolutely convulsed with roaring laughter. Perhaps you should have been there to properly appreciate the situation. It was incredible!"

• • •

Bruce eventually decided to go freelance. We had been talking about it for some time and I encouraged him to go for it. We always talked things over and made decisions together. Lots of people wanted to work with him: studio owners, musicians, record label people. We had a lot of friends in the business by now and it was time for Bruce to choose who he'd record.

At first, when the phone didn't ring, he would ask his mom to please call to make sure the phone was working. The kids and I mailed Bruce's new calling card to prospective clients. This consisted of a five-inch tape box with two wrinkled pieces of quarter-inch recording tape held together by a crooked piece of splicing tape. The box cover said "A sample of my work." Of course, that got many laughs and a strong response, and once again he was working day and night. At this point I started handling the business side of things, which I still do to this day, over fifty years later. Booking, billing, bookkeeping, lawyers and travel arrangements kept me busy.

It was at Paragon where Bruce met Ed Cherney. Ed was applying for a job as an assistant engineer. The application consisted of questions about music recording, and he was in the lounge deep in thought as he filled it out. Bruce happened to walk by and asked him if he needed any help. "That'd be great!" replied Ed. But being the scamp that he was, Bruce gave him all the incorrect answers to the questions. Despite that prank, Ed got the job and later served as Bruce's assistant engineer on Michael Jackson's *Off the Wall* and Quincy Jones' *The Dude* albums, as well as on sessions for Lena Horne, Chaka Khan and many other artists. Eddie loved working with Bruce, and was quoted as saying that "I was a human sponge sitting next to him." He went on to enjoy tremendous success in LA working with Bonnie Raitt, Willie Nelson, Bob Dylan, and the Rolling Stones, to name a few.

Building Sound Market Studios. Bruce knew how everything worked.

Around this time, Bruce also designed Sound Market Studios on North Michigan Avenue for Dick Marx. They had originally called it "Eight Track Studios" but soon after the opening, eight-track tape started becoming obsolete.

When a nine-foot Steinway grand piano was delivered to the studio it had to be lifted up to the eleventh floor by a crane, which really annoyed the shoppers on North Michigan Avenue as half of the street was closed for hours. It was here that Bruce started working with the Chi-Lites, who would later be famous for their many hits.

One day when Bruce was busy working at with Dick, I got a call from them. Excitedly they told me, "Get someone to stay with the kids for a few days—we're all going to Vegas tonight! Our flight leaves at 10 PM." Within minutes I had talked some friends of ours into coming to stay with our three teenagers as well as Hans, our Great Dane, and two cats.

I threw some clothes into a suitcase, rushed to the bank to get some cash, and got on the Chicago Northwestern into the city to meet everyone. The group included our hosts, Dick and Ruth Marx, Frank 'Porky' and Claire Panico, and Jean Gruyer and his wife, plus Bruce and me, all flying first-class to Fun City, or was it 'Sin City' back then? Jean Gruyer was a composer and the musical director of the Paris Lido cabaret show, and he was working with Dick and Bruce at the time. Porky was a trumpet player and arranger who also worked with Dick. After we settled into our suites at the beautiful Dunes Hotel and had a dip in the pool, we cleaned up and enjoyed a late dinner, after which we headed to the Sands where Jean and all of us had a stage-front table. The entertainers were none other than The Rat Pack: Frank Sinatra, Dean Martin, Sammy Davis Jr., Joey Bishop, and Peter Lawford. What an unbelievable experience—a once in a lifetime thrill!

We would play the gaming tables and generally hang out till dawn. One night I was playing at the roulette table when this well–known comedian (I won't name names) invited me to his room for a drink. "Fantastic!" I replied. "I'll just ask my husband to join us." His answer was to just walk away. Ah, show biz!

• • •

Bruce recorded the famed Muddy Waters album *Live at Mr. Kelly's* in 1971. It included the song "Boom Boom," composed by the legendary John Lee Hooker. In 1975 Bruce recorded the young Natalie Cole's album *Inseparable* for Capitol Records at Universal. She won two Grammy Awards for that album as Best New Artist and Best Female R&B Vocal Performance.

Mr. Kelly's and the London House were sold to a corporation in 1969 and closed in 1975. The number of bands and acts that always stopped in Chicago for club dates became less and less. Music was changing and bands were playing a different kind of music, touring and playing big stadiums, not nightclubs, and late night TV kept people at home. For the recording scene local talent was now where it was at.

• • •

Bruce met record producer Carl Davis back in 1962 at Universal when they recorded the hit "Duke of Earl" with Gene Chandler. Bruce loved that song. It was later inducted into the Grammy Hall of Fame and the Rock and Roll Hall of Fame as one of "The Songs that Shaped Rock and Roll."

Carl and Bruce hit it off right away. In 1970 Carl and Nat Tarnapol, owners of Brunswick Records, would ask Bruce to design and help build a studio in a building they owned on South Michigan Avenue… which he was very happy to do. We were friends with everyone who worked there and would often have them over for dinner at our home in Highland Park.

That studio played a big part in creating the sound of "Chicago Soul." Carl had a reputation as a "hitpicker" and lived up to that name many times over. He and Bruce would go on to do the Chi-Lites' "Oh Girl" and "Have You Seen Her," Tyrone Davis's "Turn Back the Hands of Time," Jackie Wilson's "Your Love Keeps Lifting Me Higher" and many more hit singles. Bruce loved the gang at Brunswick and they loved him. The work he did there would influence his sound for the rest of his career.

He remembered those years this way: *"We really did some very unique things with the Chi-Lites. That's where I began experimenting with moving the singers in closer and away from the microphone when we overdubbed the harmonies. That technique greatly affected the sound of Michael Jackson's* Thriller. *I got that sound in my ear. It started with the Chi-Lites in Chicago."*

Eugene Record of the Chi-Lites at Brunswick

• • •

Roberta has her own memories of the era. "I was studying at Sherwood Music School on South Michigan Avenue," she recalls, "and would walk down to the Brunswick studio to hang with my dad and go home to the suburbs together. The neighborhood was a little rough around the edges, but the music in that building was stunning: hot grooves and soft, sweet ballads."

In his twenty years in the Minneapolis and Chicago studios Bruce had recorded many of the greatest artists in American music history: Duke Ellington, Woody Herman, Stan Kenton, Julie London, Ramsey Lewis, Tommy and Jimmy Dorsey, Gene Chandler, Lionel Hampton, John Lee Hooker, Herbie Hancock, Curtis Mayfield, Muddy Waters, Frankie Valli and the Four Seasons, Louis Prima, Keely Smith, Dinah Shore, Herbie Mann, Les Brown, Art Blakey, Count Basie, Sarah Vaughan, Oscar Peterson, Dinah Washington, Buddy Miles, Barbara Acklin, Tyrone Davis, Chi-Lites, Jackie Wilson, James Mack, Johnny Janis, The St. Olaf Choir, Ralph Shapey, The Chicago Symphony Orchestra and more.

• • •

Bruce and me with Eddie Harris

Over the years Bruce recorded many albums with innovative fusion composer/saxophonist Eddie Harris, including the well known *Exodus to Jazz*, the first gold jazz album ever recorded at Universal. We had become friends with Eddie and his wife Sally, who had recently moved to Los Angeles and were encouraging us to do the same. Eddie was adamant that Bruce still engineer his records, so we made a trip to LA, where Bruce would record the album *Bad Luck Is All I Have*. Eddie loved crazy song titles like "That Is Why You're Overweight," "I Need Some Money," "How Can You Live Like That," and "The Reason Why I'm Talking S–T!". In LA, he and Bruce mainly worked at the Village Recorder in West Hollywood. This was the studio built by Geordie Hormel, who Bruce knew from working on projects in Minneapolis at our old studio, and whose family made the Spam my family ate in the Naga Hills. Bruce and Eddie always enjoyed working together and had a shared sense of humor. I came with Bruce on this trip and we stayed with Eddie and Sally in their beautiful home in the Hollywood hills, and had a wonderful time. She was perfect for him, and they adored each other. After long days in the studio Bruce and Eddie would relax in the pool. Tragically, Eddie died when he was only 62. I am still in touch with Sally and their daughters.

It didn't take long before Quincy heard Bruce was in town. He remembered him well from the Dinah Washington days and called him to work on his next project, which was an album for Lesley Gore called *Love Me By Name*. Quincy had produced the 17-year old Lesley's big hit "It's My Party" in 1963 for Mercury Records, which had shot up to #1 on the Billboard Hot 100. He brought on some serious players for this new album, including Herbie Hancock, Toots Thielemans, Harvey Mason, and Dave Grusin. And now he had Bruce back at the board. The magic was ready to begin again.

One day in 1976, shortly before we relocated, Bruce ran into songwriter and singer Jerry Butler, along with Carl Davis, guitarist Phil Upchurch, and some other Chicago notables in a studio hallway and Jerry said in his "cool as ice" baritone voice: "Bruce, we hear you're going to Hollywood on us. Nothin' wrong with that. But don't forget, we taught you everything you know. Now you're goin' to LA and *they* will discover *you*." Bruce later wrote: "That's exactly what happened. Jerry was certainly right on that score!"

Chicago had been very good to us, that's for sure. We were just kids when we got there and that big, wonderful, musical city took us on a ride for two decades that changed us forever. Bruce said of his time there, "The years in Chicago were extremely happy, very musical years. I was definitely in the right place at the right time."

But now it was time to move on.

CHAPTER FOUR

LOS ANGELES

I found a lovely house for us in Woodland Hills, about a half hour drive from LA.

The kids were all in their twenties by now and out of the house doing their own things. Driving from Chicago to California was an adventure. Everything was on its way in huge moving vans. I had shipped my two horses, Susie and Willie. I was in the Oldsmobile with Hans the Great Dane and our two Siamese cats, Christie and Captain Bligh; Bruce was driving the Ford Bronco packed full of gear. Communication was tricky—this was before cell phones. But we had CB radios. Somewhere in St. Louis, Bruce took a wrong turn. Before long, a couple of truckers heard me trying to tell Bruce how to get back on the highway. I told him I would wait for him at the next truck stop. The truckers helped us find each other and gave us handles. I was 'Viking Lady,' Bruce was 'Tugboat,' and Hans the dog was 'Tomato Paste' because they thought his name was 'Hunts.' The truckers said they had never heard of a lost man who was so eager to find his wife! We all finally met at the truck stop and these same truckers treated us to lunch. They were truly modern day cowboys.

With my dear Susie

LA felt comfortable right from the start. I finally had my horses at home, with beautiful stalls in my own barn to house Susie and Willie. And no snow and ice! One time in Chicago I had to dig ice out of Susie's hoof with my car keys. Never again. Sunny skies, not too hot, not too cold. Just right.

We had a corporation now, which I was handling. Bruce wasn't at all interested in the business end of things. All he cared about was the music and the artists. I was happy to do it. We had been partners from the start.

"To min 'store Bror' (my big brother). I love you, Quincy"

Bruce was in seventh heaven working with Quincy once again, and vice versa. Quincy's second wife Ulla was Swedish, so they had a connection and could banter some Swedish phrases back and forth in the studio. Quincy had gigged in Sweden in the 50's and had two kids with Ulla: Tina and Quincy III. Bruce and Quincy called each other "Svensk" and "Jones." Their shared sense of humor and love of food was legendary.

They also had some serious classical music in their backgrounds, Bruce from his parents and his own playing and singing, and Quincy, who had studied in Paris with composition guru Nadia Boulanger, who was also the teacher of composers Aaron Copland and Leonard Bernstein and a friend of Ravel and Stravinsky.

Bruce and Quincy had a legendary telepathy in the studio, reading each other's minds about what was needed when. Along with a musical integrity and drive about how to get it to the people, they both deeply believed in communicating what they called "the emotion of the music," as described in this 2012 article by music journalist Matthew Allen:

Soul and Science: The Partnership of Quincy Jones and Bruce Swedien

"Presentation is just as important as the product itself. A succulent steak dinner isn't as appetizing if it's served on the back of a garbage can lid. In music this is a principle that is largely taken for granted but overwhelmingly essential to understand.

A great song cannot be a great song without great execution. Aside from the artist, it needs a producer to choose the proper personnel and mold the music as it best serves the material. In addition, it is the engineer's responsibility to capture the performance in its proper sonic context.

Quincy Jones has earned the distinction of being the greatest producer in music history, mostly due to his collaboration with Michael

Jackson. However, it is his pairing with someone else during that time that altered and swiftly defined modern pop music: engineer Bruce Swedien.

Between 1976 and 1995, the duo of Jones and Swedien generated platinum- selling records for Jackson, George Benson, Rufus, Chaka Khan, Donna Summer and many others, thanks to their perfect marriage of spontaneity and calculation. Quincy offered his gift for arranging and orchestrating compositions in order to fulfill its melodic and rhythmic potential. Bruce contributed his extraordinary way of mixing, using ... special microphones and other unorthodox methods [of] maximizing the sonic potential of a recording.

The partnership between Quincy Jones and Bruce Swedien was conceived in 1959. They met at Universal Studios in Chicago, both working on a session for [the] Queen of the Blues, Dinah Washington. That session spawned five records, including the top ten Grammy winning hit, "What a Diff'rence a Day Makes."

Their presence at that session speaks to a reoccurring resource that each would use, in radical fashion, to record their commercial smashes later: Jazz. Jones' pedigree in jazz is well documented. He learned trumpet from Clark Terry, charting from Ray Charles, and played with Lionel Hampton, Dizzy Gillespie and Billie Holiday.

Bruce's background as an engineer was also rich in the medium, having worked with Duke Ellington, Art Blakey and the Jazz Messengers, and others. From that point, Jones and Swedien clicked instantly. They'd work together periodically for the next 20 years with artists like Washington and Count Basie.

In 1977, Jones invited Swedien to work with him on a movie musical he was scoring and supervising. Swedien jumped at the chance and from that moment, they were inseparable. That movie was The Wiz, *and was the birth of a steady offspring of projects that would help shape the course of American music.*

It was during the pre-recording phase of The Wiz *that Swedien witnessed the full gauge of Jones' uncanny and unparalleled prowess* as a producer. Jones amassed a prestigious lineup of singers and jazz musicians to take Charlie Smalls' score—Jones composed five new songs as well—to a zenith that would be unrivaled by other musicals: Ron Carter, Ralph McDonald, Hubert Laws, Harvey Mason, Bob James, Roberta Flack, Luther Vandross, Cissy Houston, and so on.

Jones explained his methodology in his documentary Quincy Jones: The Many Lives of Q: "I listen to the orchestra like an x-ray machine because I've been around it all my life. That's what I do. If it's too thick, too thin, too slow or too fast, wrong key or whatever it is, all I have to do is just listen, and I hear it."

The Wiz would prove to be the template for the two going forward.

On their next project, Jones' 1978 solo release Sounds… and Stuff Like That (featuring Vandross, Chaka Khan and Herbie Hancock), Swedien developed a system of multitrack multiplexing that utilized double stereo microphone recordings, designed exclusively for his work with Jones. This method would later be known as the Acusonic Recording Process, a clever combination of "accurate" and "sonic" coined by Jones and Michael Jackson. Swedien explained further at a 1984 NARAS luncheon: "The 'accurate' part of it referred to the accuracy of the true stereophonic sound imagery; the 'sonic' part of it referred to the fact that it is sound that we are trying to characterize."

The Process is the practice of recording into two or more multitrack tape machines so that you could have a nearly unlimited number of tracks. This allowed Swedien to get a "more genuine stereophonic image" instead of a stereo sound simulated by monophonic manipulation, not to mention preventing the master tracks from being played too much during the overdubbing process. In the end, the song's sound was not only crystal clear, but exuded a sphere of sound rather than a wall of sound, giving the listener a virtually live experience.

Within the comfort of the Acusonic Recording Process, Quincy was able to really stretch his imagination in the studio. He assembled an "A-Team" of musicians to use during his and Bruce's sessions: Rufus drummer JR Robinson, Brothers Johnson bassist Louis Johnson, keyboardist Greg Phillinganes, Toto guitarist Steve Lukather, percussionist Paulinho da Costa, and trumpet player Jerry Hey. Jones continued to fuse his jazz arranging skills into the pop context, approaching each album like his big band LPs in the 1950s and 1960s (i.e. 1969's Walking in Space), giving the material more urgency and poignancy.

Another key element in Jones and Swedien's success was constant risk taking. For his 1981 album The Dude, Jones recruited Ray Charles keyboardist James Ingram… as a vocalist. After hearing him sing on a demo, Ingram was brought to the studio to lend his gruff, masculine timbre to the title track and the ballads "Just Once" and "One Hundred Ways," earning Ingram his first Grammy.

Bruce Swedien also found ways to get that something extra out of a recording. During the Off the Wall sessions, Swedien built a short plywood drum platform to minimize the seepage of reverb into neighboring instrument tracks, thus richen its power ([the] best example is on "Rock With You"). He decided to let Michael Jackson stand on top of the platform in the recording booth while recording lead vocals. This captured all the rhythmic non-vocal nuances of Jackson's dancing, hand claps and finger snaps into the track. Jackson recorded with that platform for the rest of his career.

Part of Swedien's genius was the fact that he didn't have to follow the engineer "rule book" to the letter and always stayed open minded to come up with unique ways to enhance a recording. "I will always sacrifice a technical value for a production value," Swedien stated in his autobiography Make Mine Music. "If I were looking for a very 'breathy,' sensuous vocal sonic image, for instance, I would place the singer as close as physically possible to the microphone, thereby eliminating almost all early reflections. I would even use no windscreen, if possible."

At the end of the mixing stage, Jones and Swedien both wanted to make sure that the public would not only get off on the power of the music's performance and emotions, but also appreciate the sound quality. It was crucial that the music had sonic clarity, shine and impact that enhanced the quality of the already beautiful music.

In The Many Lives of Q *documentary, Toto guitarist and A-Team member Steve Lukather talked about the duo's philosophy during Michael Jackson's* Thriller *sessions: "We'd do a track and of course you come back and they put it on the big speakers and it sounds all big and huge. Then Quincy would say, 'put it on the radio,' because he wanted to see if it had the same vibe." If the listener got the same impact through small speakers as they did through big ones, then the recording was finished.*

By the end of the century, Quincy Jones and Bruce Swedien were a two-headed cultural conglomerate; responsible for countless million sellers and #1 singles, including Rufus' "Do You Love What You Feel," George Benson's "Give Me the Night," Patti Austin's "Baby Come to Me," Michael Jackson's "Billie Jean," The Brothers Johnson's "Stomp," Quincy's "The Secret Garden," James Ingram's "Yah Mo Be There," Jones and Tamia's "You Put a Move On My Heart," and a score of others. To this day, digital recording programs like Pro Tools fight to live up to the duo's clairvoyant approach to analog recording.

Their success wasn't just based on talent, intuitiveness and ingenuity, but also on friendship, admiration, and respect for each other and the music. "We had the perfect balance of soul and science— it's always about that," Jones stated in his book, Q on Producing. *'There's always a science behind the passion and fire in music—it's what enables the artist to fully unleash his or her creativity. People think it's all about nature's innate talent. No way!"*

Bruce summed up the relationship this way:

"I think the way Quincy and I work in the studio is a bit unique—a lot of people comment when they see Quincy and I working in the studio that we don't talk much. I guess we really don't. When you really think about it, we've been working together so long, that a lot of it is just like a sixth sense. We know how each other's minds work. One of the things

that's really important to me is that we have a lot of fun while we're doing a project—and I think it shows in the music. The fact that we both dearly love good food is important to the way we relate to each other. Quincy says that all the good food that we have in the studio goes in the music.

A lot of our conversation, for instance, the way Quincy describes musical values, is to use culinary terms. . . . For instance, Quincy will say: "OK, that sounds great . . . but add a little spice to that sound or add a little garlic salt or something," and instinctively I'll know what he's talking about.

When Quincy asks me to make the sound a little spicy, it means add a little bit of high end, or you might want to add a harmonizer to the sound source, or add a little special effect to it or something. Q has told me that the music will tell you when it needs a bit of garlic salt.

Sometimes when we work on a project, if we are really fortunate, Quincy will take it upon himself to personally fix our lunch. It didn't happen very often but when it did, what a great experience!

For instance, it takes Quincy 45 minutes to make a chicken sandwich—he'll get the chicken—have it sent over from Greenblatt's Deli or somewhere, and get the butter and the mayo. Then he'll take a piece of bread, and spread the butter and mayo, very, very carefully on every little square inch of the bread. He goes about that just the way he does with his music. Every square millimeter is perfectly covered with butter and mayo. Then the chicken has to be all torn apart in exactly the same sized little pieces, and fitted just right on the bread. Quincy Jones makes the best chicken sandwich in life! Somehow Quincy's approach to music always made great sense to me, once I'd had the privilege of watching Quincy Jones fix a chicken sandwich. It's the same for music or a chicken sandwich for Quincy. It's all about the details.

Everything good that I've learned about recording music, or about the ethics of music, came from my experiences with Quincy Jones. Especially about the aesthetics of musical quality. I'm a very fortunate guy, I went to the University of Quincy Jones! If you think about it, who else is there like Quincy?"

They started their LA journey with the soundtrack to "Roots," the star-studded ABC television series in 1977 from the Alex Haley book, set during and after the time of slavery in the United States. This was an extremely important project for Quincy. He researched the history of African music and really poured his heart into those scores. "Roots" won many, many awards, including an Emmy for the music.

Then it was the Brothers Johnson album *Blam*—a blend of funk, R&B, jazz, and pop that topped the charts. Quincy and Bruce also did their album *Light Up The Night* in 1980, another chart topper. They were on a lot of Quincy projects through the years. He called Louis, the bass player, "Thunder Thumbs" and George, the guitarist, was "Electric Licks." They were both talented musicians but they didn't always get along, to put it mildly. They often wouldn't speak to each other. In the studio! George would say "Bruce, tell Louis this" and Bruce would tell Louis, and then Louis would say "Bruce, tell George that" and Bruce would tell George.

Somewhere I have a photo of me riding on one of my horses with a T-shirt that says "Get the Funk Out Ma Face."

• • •

Next was Quincy's album *Sounds and Stuff Like That* with Patti Austin, Ashford and Simpson, Chaka Khan, Stevie Wonder, Herbie Hancock, Luther Vandross, Michael McDonald, Hubert Laws, and Steve Gadd. This would be our new normal, a roomful of stellar artists, with Bruce at the console and Quincy inspiring everyone. I was at many of those sessions, hanging out with these amazing musicians, our new friends. It was the beginning of a family that would last for years and years. It was different from the scene in Chicago: friendlier, freer, less guarded. Danish engineer Niels Erik Lund was Bruce's assistant on *Sounds* and remembers "the kind and highly professional atmosphere that filled the room." That's what it was: warmth and greatness. Needless to say, Bruce and Quincy were on a serious roll. We were going with the flow once again, ready for anything.

•   •   •

Peggy Lipton was the love of Quincy's life. They were happily married and had two beautiful daughters, Rashida and Kidada. We hit it off right from the moment we first met. We went to parties, traveled and laughed a lot together. She had a great sense of humor, was very down to earth, and was a loving mom to the girls. Peggy had been a model and actress on TV's "The Mod Squad" and later, "Twin Peaks." But she stopped her career when she and Quincy had their kids, both of whom went on to become actresses themselves. Rashida has been in such hits as "Boston Public," "The Office" and "Parks and Recreation," and she made a moving Netflix documentary about Quincy that won the Grammy Award for Best Music Film in 2019.

•   •   •

Bruce and Quincy on the set of "The Wiz"

One night the phone rang quite late. It was Quincy. Bruce was relaxing in the bathtub. I brought him the phone. Pretty soon I heard him yell, "Hell yes! When do we start?" Quincy wanted him to go to New York to work on the movie musical *The Wiz*.

So, off to New York where Quincy and Bruce were going to be roommates, sharing a suite at the Drake Hotel. Talk about the odd couple. Bruce took care of getting the laundry and Q ordered the food and wine. Actor Telly Savalas, who starred in the hit 70s TV show "Kojak" had occupied the suite shortly before Bruce and Quincy had moved in. Consequently, on several occasions a lovely young lady or two would knock on the door in the wee hours looking for "Mr. Savalas."

The Wiz was a movie version of the Broadway musical of the same name. It was an African-American take on the classic *Wizard of Oz* by Frank Baum set in modern day New York.

The filming took place at Astoria Studios in Queens and on location throughout New York City. It was a stellar group, with Sidney Lumet directing, Lena Horne as Glinda the Good Witch, Diana Ross as Dorothy, Nipsey Russell as the Tin Man, Ted Ross as the Cowardly Lion, Richard Pryor as the Wizard and, of course, the nineteen-year-old Michael Jackson as the scarecrow.

That's where I first met Michael, on the set of *The Wiz*. He was truly a gentle soul. Well-mannered, humble, polite, he always said "Please" and "Thank you." He was such a sweet young man, so quiet, a great listener, sincere and professional.

His talent was unbelievable, as everyone knows. But to see it right in front of you, sometimes in the same room when he was trying a vocal idea was like being in another world. He was so focused, always paying attention and ridiculously prepared. He knew every word to every song in the show.

The entire cast was so friendly and took us in like we were part of the show, part of the crew. Once again, I was accepted with open arms. You know, for the most part, the higher up you go, the nicer people are.

Bruce with Lena Horne as Glinda the Good Witch in "The Wiz"

Working with Q, Sidney and that incredible cast plus all the amazing musicians was the thrill of a lifetime and some of the best times one could have working on a major motion picture production. I especially enjoyed visiting with Sidney, as during World War II he had been stationed in Chabua, a town in Assam, India, close to where I had grown up. We both remembered the elegant restaurant Firpo's in Calcutta from the days of the British Raj. I had been there, but only for tea as we were just missionaries, but Sidney had dined there more than once. There was a ballroom with an orchestra for dancing and a delicious five-course dinner. Your napkin was put in your lap by a maître d' in black tie and tails and behind your chair were hovering waiters in turbans, white gloves, and white tunics with gold trim. At the next table you might find a *Maharaja* and his bejeweled *Maharani* or a British Field Marshal and his very British wife. Sidney and I time-traveled together and thoroughly enjoyed ourselves.

The Wiz's music was recorded at A&R Studios in New York. Poor Lena was allergic to freon so they had to turn off the air-conditioning when she was recording her vocals on "If You Believe." Her Broadway shows sold out, but the theater was cooking in the summer. And when Diana Ross was to record her vocals she asked that everyone except Bruce and Quincy leave the control room. Peggy and I were there, along with a few others. I obediently left; Peggy ignored the request.

During a break in the recording, Tom Bähler, who was also on the project, asked me to come into the studio to hear a new song he had written. He sat down at the piano and played and sang his new composition.

The song was a beautiful, emotional ballad about love and regret called "She's Out of My Life," which would eventually appear on Michael's first solo album, *Off the Wall*. Of the experience, Bruce later wrote: "*Michael would break down and cry at the end of every take. We recorded six or seven takes. At the end of each take he was sobbing, actually crying. When we finished the last take, Michael was too*

embarrassed to come into the control room. He just tippy-toed out of
the back door of the studio, got in his car, and left the studio building."

On one visit I made to New York, Bruce and the movie's sound crew
had assembled a location truck for playback for the dancers. This time
it was for the "Poppy Girls" scene. The location was just off Eighth
Avenue in New York. I was in the sound truck when we heard some
yelling and pounding under the floor. It was a couple of winos that had
moved in under the truck and I guess the music was keeping them
awake. We did find it necessary to call on some of New York's finest
to remove these guys because they had started a fire to keep themselves
warm.

When Sidney decided on the location for the Emerald City scene,
there were no other options in his mind—it was to be shot on the street
level of the World Trade Center. It was November and it was cold and
I felt sorry for the scantily dressed dancers. I believe there were at least
five hundred in the cast and crew. We were all fed a delicious turkey
dinner by the caterers. How very sad that the lady who was a
photographer on the project, Berry Berenson, was killed on that very
same spot when the plane she was on flew into the Twin Towers on
9/11.

Quincy loved to work at night. We all remember one occasion in
particular. There were eighty musicians scheduled for a recording
session the next day to record the overture for *The Wiz* and Q had not
written a note. Typical of Quincy! He sat at the dining room table in
their suite at the Drake at 9 PM and worked all night. No piano, no
guitar, not necessary—the sound was in his head. The next morning,
Bruce woke up and went into the dining room and there was Quincy
surrounded by sheets of music, just finishing up. They went to the
studio where a team of copyists was ready and waiting to furiously copy
the parts for the session. And it was perfect, gorgeous music.

After many months, the film was completed. We had a wrap party
at Windows of the World, the restaurant on the top floor of the World

Trade Center. What a thrill to be a part of this important project, and to get to meet some of the nicest people you can imagine.

• • •

It was time to get ready to start work on *Off the Wall*. After working with Quincy on *The Wiz*, Michael knew he wanted Q to produce it.

Quincy, Rod Temperton and Bruce the day they started "Off the Wall"

Sessions for the album were booked at Cherokee, Allen Zentz, and Westlake Studios in LA. It was great working with Q as well as with Rod Temperton, whom we had just met. Of course, his reputation as a composer and musician was well known, but if you knew Rod, you wouldn't imagine he could write such huge hits. He lived a reclusive life in London with his wife and was the furthest thing from Hollywood glitz and glamor imaginable. But he had a marvelous sense of humor and a legendary work ethic. During one session, he had a horrible toothache so he found a pair of pliers, pulled his tooth out, and kept working. Not your average guy.

Rod's wife, Kathy Buckley Temperton and I really hit it off from the start. There's something about the kinship of being "studio wives" that created a lasting friendship. She is the dearest, sweetest person. She is from England, as is Rod, had been around the business for ages, and was devoted to Rod. She loved to travel. And travel we did. One of our trips was to Cabo San Lucas in Baja, California. We visited our old boating friends Mickey and Randy Short, and thoroughly enjoyed exploring, listening to Mariachi bands, and just relaxing. And in 1992 Kathy, Roberta, my brother Jim and I went to Indonesia together.

For *Off the Wall*, Rod had just flown in from London, arriving the morning of the first session. He brought three songs with him for Quincy and Michael to choose from: "Rock With You," "Off the Wall," and "Burn This Disco Out." They chose all three and a longtime relationship started then and there. Later, Quincy, Bruce, and Rod would be known as "The Dream Team." Quincy's A-team of musicians included Greg Phillinganes on keyboards, Louis Johnson on bass, John "JR" Robinson on drums, Steve Lukather on guitar, and Paulhino da Costa, a Brazilian percussionist, along with trumpeter and arranger Jerry Hey. There were many more musicians on Quincy's sessions, of course, but these guys played most of them. It was a tight group that Quincy called his "Killer Q posse." When *Off the Wall* was released, Quincy had huge awards made for all of them, spray painted to look like actual graffiti.

Michael won the first-ever 3M Scotty Award for Off The Wall

Michael had a subtle sense of humor. His jokes and pranks were silly, childlike, innocent, and unsophisticated… and he liked to play tricks on you. He would say something like, "Look, Bruce! What have you spilled on your shirt?" After he caught you looking down, he'd giggle and leave the room.

We knew Michael since he was 19 years old, and never once did we see anything remotely close to inappropriate behavior. What the liars, lawyers, and press accused him of is unforgivable, criminal. People who knew Michael knew he could never have done those horrible things. Friends, family, and colleagues who had known Michael for decades were in shock at the accusations and public humiliation and disgrace that he was put through. Michael was a gentle, generous loving human being.

Michael won the Best R&B Vocal Performance award at the 1980 Grammys, and to date *Off the Wall* has sold over 20 million copies worldwide, making it one of the best-selling albums of all time.

Bruce's assistants on this project were Steve Conger and Rick Ash. One weekend while we were on our boat in Channel Island harbor we received a horrific phone call. Steve was dead! We were devastated by this news. According to the news reports, this was the scenario: Steve lived in an apartment on Fairfax Avenue, just down the street from Cherokee Studios. Next door to his apartment building was a motel. Apparently there had been an aggressive argument between some people in the parking lot of the motel. Steve noticed it was getting physically violent so he went into a nearby phone booth to call the police. The first policeman on the scene was a young rookie cop. He assumed that Steve was a part of the mayhem and promptly shot and killed poor, sweet Steve. His death was totally uncalled for. He was just trying to get help. What a great loss! Bruce was absolutely distraught. We were all in shock. Not long after, I was called for jury duty. The case in question was one of police brutality against four young Latino guys. Needless to say, I was not assigned to that jury. It was so hard to go back to the project after the shooting. Bruce would see Steve's apartment from the parking lot every day.

• • •

The band Rufus, with Chaka Khan as lead singer, originally came from Chicago. JR Robinson played drums in the band, and both he and Chaka would be in the studio with Quincy on many projects. In 1979 he produced their album *Masterjam*. Bruce engineered and mixed, Rod wrote a song, Jerry Hey played trumpet, and Louis Johnson was on bass. It was the gang once again. The album went platinum and was at the top of the R & B and pop charts. We were getting used to this!

The next project was George Benson's album *Give Me the Night*. Quincy produced, Rod wrote the title song and the track "Love X Love," and Bruce recorded and mixed the entire album. Herbie Hancock, Patti Austin, Greg Phillinganes, Jerry Hey, and Michael Boddicker all played on it.

Word had gotten out about the project and pretty soon I got a call from Kendun Studios in Burbank. The caller was promoting their studio, saying, "We have seven couches in our lounge and I just know Max, your large Great Dane, would love being here." I don't know if this is why Bruce and Quincy decided to record George's album there. Since I was scheduled to be in San Diego at around that time with my friend and horse trainer Karen Kittleson and our beautiful palomino horse, Willie, at the Del Mar National Horse Show, Bruce became Max's nanny. Every day the two of them went to Kendun to work, along with Max's blanket, food and doggie treats. (Max had decided to heck with all those fancy couches in the lounge.)

Bruce with Max, the studio dog

Bruce recounted: *"Our first stop, on the way to the studio, was at McDonalds for a few quarter-pounder hamburgers for breakfast. We both loved them with cheese. I ate one; Max ate four. Max watched me carefully as I meticulously removed the pickles from his quarter-pounders. (Max detested pickles on his food!) After devouring our breakfast, we headed for the big, beautiful city park in Burbank. Max had to have his walk and do his doggie duties. After our brief visit to the park we headed straight for Kendun Studios. Once there, we settled in for a long day in the studio. I filled Max's water dish and put his blanket down in a cozy corner of the control room. By this time in his life Max was used to long, drawn-out days in the studio. He didn't seem to mind at all. I have a feeling he really enjoyed the music.*

I got started and pretty soon Quincy came in and said hello to Max and everyone else in the control room. We started editing and mixing. The song was "Moody's Mood For Love." My recording format, in those days was, of course, 24 track analog tape. After a while Marty Paich came in to hear the song. Marty did the string arrangement on "Moody's Mood For Love," and was going to conduct the orchestra for the string session. Marty was a top-drawer bonafide dog lover, so before we could start, he had to get down on his hands and knees and give Max his props.

George had finished his guitar parts and had sung the lead vocal. Patti Austin had done her fantastic vocal the day before. The following day we were set to record the strings. Marty made some notes as I played the song for him a couple of times. Marty said goodbye to us, patted Max on the head and left the studio.

We had to make sure that the 24-track tapes were absolutely as perfect as we could make them. Quincy said to me, "Play the tapes from the second verse, that's where the strings will enter. I want to make absolutely sure what Greg Phillinganes played there."

I hit the Play button on the master 24-track tape machine to run both the master and the slave 24-track machines. Nothing happened. My heart sank to my feet! I hit Play again. Nothing! Oh boy. . . . I looked at Quincy. Q looked at me with one of his knowing looks. . . . I told Quincy, "We had better take a little break while I get this sorted out." Without blinking, Quincy announced to everyone in the control room, "Hey guys, Bruce is going to have another one of his AES (Audio Engineering Society) meetings!" That got a big laugh!

After two hours of messing with those two 24-track machines that didn't want to work with each other, I noticed some quiet little snoring sounds coming from the corner of the control room. Interesting, I thought to myself. . . the snoring was in two distinct pitches. I looked over and there was Quincy and Max, curled up together, sound asleep, in the corner of the control room on Max's beautiful soft, red blanket. Later, Max did get a mention in Rolling Stone *magazine and George's album went on to become a huge success."*

Karen Kittleson and Willie

And Willie, my beautiful Palomino, did win reserve champion. He was a character. He once stole Karen's truck keys out of her back pocket! Five of my horsey friends, two dogs, and a trailer with Willie and his companion horse. Brian Gardner, who is a well known mastering engineer at Bernie Grundman Mastering Engineers, joined us at Del Mar along with his family to video the competition, as did my brother Jim and his wife Marlys. Brian was such a big fan of Max's that he had "Max" put on the vinyl of the Rufus and Chaka Khan album *Masterjam*.

• • •

Next was 1981's platinum-selling *The Dude*, featuring the memorable song "Razzamatazz" sung by Patti Austin, as well as the hits "Just Once" and "One Hundred Ways" with James Ingram. By this point, Bruce and Quincy had assembled a perfect group of musicians: Rufus drummer JR Robinson, Brothers Johnson bassist Louis Johnson, keyboardist Greg Phillinganes, guitarist Steve Lukather, percussionist Paulhino da Costa, synth player Michael Boddicker and trumpet player Jerry Hey. Rod Temperton was there composing, Tom and Michael

Bähler were singing back-up vocals, and Herbie Hancock and Stevie Wonder made guest appearances as well. Only Quincy could assemble a group like that. Wonderful Ed Cherney from the Chicago days assisted Bruce on the project. We were a family. The album was nominated for twelve Grammy Awards and won three.

• • •

I loved bringing treats to that loveable and hard-working crew. And boy, did they deserve it! I would load up the back of our Suburban with all sorts of home-cooked delights. But their favorites were always my Swedish meatballs and sugar cookies. See for yourself:

Swedish Meatballs
Mix in a bowl: 1 egg, 2 slices of bread, ½ cup of milk
Add: 1 lb. ground beef, 1 chopped onion
1 tsp ground allspice, 1 ½ tsp salt
Roll into small balls, brown in butter
When browned add about 1 cup water
Simmer for 30 minutes, covered
Thicken pan gravy with 1 tbsp flour & water

(Bruce loved Swedish meatballs with mashed potatoes and gravy, peas and cottage cheese with Swedish Lingonberries.)

Sugar Cookies
Mix in a large bowl: 1 cup each of:
Sugar, powdered sugar, butter, vegetable oil
1 tsp soda, 1 tsp vanilla, ½ tsp salt, 2 eggs
Add 4 ¼ cups flour
Chill dough
Roll dough into balls the size of walnuts
Place on an ungreased cookie sheet
Flatten with the bottom of a glass dipped in sugar
Bake at 350° for 10-12 minutes

• • •

Quincy and Peggy, along with their two girls, plus Rod and Kathy Temperton, Patti Austin, met Bruce and I in Worms, Germany, where Rod and Kathy lived at the time. We were all going to Nice, where we had chartered a gorgeous yacht to sail to Monaco.

While in Worms we had a blast. It was the town's Wine Festival. Of course there was the usual carnival stuff such as food stands (Quincy ate eight slices of pizza), rides, etc. Peggy, Quincy, Patti, Bruce and I went on a ride called the VIKING. It was terrifying! Patti kept yelling, "I want to get off!" while Peggy wet her pants. After some recovery time, Rod and Quincy, who do not drive, got on the dodgem cars and drove like maniacs slamming into each other.

Before Bruce and I left California to fly to Worms, our sweet dog Max had cut his penis on some rebar when we were having a green house constructed. He had been bleeding off and on but the vet said not to worry. But after returning to our hotel, we phoned home only to find out that Max's condition had worsened and he needed surgery. I decided that I would fly home, stay until Max's surgery was done and then fly to Monaco to meet the rest of the gang. But Bruce refused to go on the cruise without me, so back home we flew and missed what might have been the best vacation cruise ever.

Max did recover nicely and had a very long, happy life. Quincy teased me for years afterward: "You're going home? So whose dick is broken now?"

• • •

One morning Quincy phoned me and asked if Max could come to Westlake Studio later in the day. Of course I said he'd love to. When I arrived at the studio there was Michael Jackson's chimpanzee Bubbles as well as Steven Spielberg and his young son, whose name is also Max. Steven shot some videos of Max, Max, and Bubbles. Unfortunately I neglected to ask for a copy of "Max's Film"—his debut with Spielberg behind the camera!

• • •

Soon after, Bruce was back in New York recording Lena Horne's *The Lady and Her Music* Broadway concert at the Nederlander Theater. The album was for Quincy's record label Qwest. The huge sound truck was parked in front of the theater, and the recordings went well. However, one night while Lena was onstage, there was a loud gasp from the audience so Lena went to the front of the stage not knowing the cause and then there was a loud crash as one of the enormous light bars fell onto the stage directly in back of her. Apparently the audience had seen it breaking loose and fortunately Lena had gone to the front of the stage to see what was happening. Thank God, as it saved her life! On a couple of occasions she wasn't happy with her vocal so after the concert we would all go to the studio and she would overdub vocals till 3 AM. She was such a warm and wonderful person. Of course we knew her from the *Wiz* days. Such a pro with a great sense of humor. During a break I talked about my Palomino Willy and his recent horse show conquests. After that, whenever there was a clam in the take or a technical problem, she would turn and say "Hey! Where's Willy?" What an incredible talent that lady was! *Newsweek* described her as "the most awesome performer to have hit Broadway in years." She and Quincy won the Grammy Award for Best Musical Show Album, and Lena won the Grammy for Best Pop Vocal Performance, Female.

• • •

Quincy had a great sense of humor too, and I loved him dearly. Like Michael, he loved pranks! One day while we were living in Los Angeles I decided to "get" him. I phoned him at home and in my best Indian accent I claimed to be a reporter from the Calcutta Statesman, an Indian newspaper. I said I wished to do an interview with him. "Call my assistant Ed Eckstine at my office," Quincy replied. "Vy vould I do dat?" I said. "Am I not speaking vit the von and only Qvincy Jones right now?" This silly conversation went on until I got the giggles. "I'm gonna get you!" Quincy roared. For a long time afterwards, whenever

Q would call and I happened to pick up the phone he would try to sound like a Latino woman.

One of Quincy's most endearing traits was to give friends nicknames. Michael's was "Smelly" because when music had a certain rhythm he liked, he called it "smelly jelly" (he didn't like to say the word "funky"). As I said, his nickname for Bruce was "Svensk," which means "Swede." Mine was "Clara," Greg Phillinganes' was "Mouse", Michael Boddicker's was "Lily." This was because when he was programming the synthesizer he would have several patch cords draped around his neck and he looked like Lily Tomlin who in her comedy act played Ernestine, the telephone operator. Peggy's nickname was "Bear." Carol Bayer Sager was "Network." (CBS!) Tom Baylor's nickname was "Nad" because Tom's complexion is extremely pale and there was a cream on the market called "Nadinola" that lightened your skin.

Whenever it was Rod, Quincy, or Bruce's birthday, I loved to send a singing telegram to the studio. I wonder if any of these singers made it to the top. Bet those poor gals were a nervous wreck singing in front of those guys.

• • •

After a few years of being in LA we moved to Moorpark, a community of farming and horses in Ventura County. We had a small five-acre property across from the Brennan ranch (owned by actor Walter Brennan) and the huge 200-acre ranch owned by Joel McCrea, the actor who said he acted so he could ranch. The house had a pool, and Bruce built a recording studio there which he now called "West Viking Studios." He finally got himself a massive bright green John Deere tractor and I got a classic white Rolls Royce we named "Snowflake."

Outdoor fun with the John Deere tractor

Bruce behind the wheel of my classic Rolls "Snowflake"

There was plenty of room for all the animals as well as my gardens of fruit trees and flowers. I made a lot of jam and preserves, as I had learned from my mother out in India. We had stables for six horses. I even took an equine veterinary course at Moorpark College and learned how to artificially inseminate a horse! My friends and I would go riding in the beautiful orange groves across the road. Michael loved horses and horseback riding. Once he and Brooke Shields came to visit and we saddled up Willy and Susie for them to ride and off they went through the groves. Rod and Kathy, Quincy, Peggy, and the girls all loved coming to our little ranch to ride and have fun.

Willie, Peggy, Rashida and Tina Jones

Gentle Susie and Kidada

I kept chickens, ducks, geese, guinea fowl (got poked in the eye by one of those), and four peacocks to remind me of India; one was an albino named Buddy (I loved the sound of their call). There were also our California Great Danes Max and Teddy, and a Border Collie named Zack, who I rescued from neighbors that didn't want him. More than twenty cats lived in their own building up the hill; I had a bumper sticker on the truck that said "Support your local cat house"! There were wandering coyotes from time to time up the hill looking for cat snacks. I would go out there at night with my WWII Italian Beretta rifle and shoot into the sky to scare them off.

I loved giving dinner parties. Indian, Swedish, California cuisine, you name it. I had a beautiful collection of soup tureens and would have dinner parties of soups. My curry was Assamese style, taught to me by our cook in India. I also would make a Swedish baked dish called *Jansson's Frestelse*, which is made of potatoes, onions, anchovies, bread crumbs, and cream. Sounds pretty awful but it is actually delicious. Quincy loved it. He loved to mess with names and would say, "Hey, Bea! Got any more of that 'Johnson's Wrestlin' Match?'"

Another time Quincy was over for dinner when my dad, the Swedish missionary Reverend Bengt Ivar Anderson, was visiting. They were outside looking at the property, when Quincy said to my dad, "Here's where your son-in-law spent his drug money." My father laughed and laughed! Fortunately.

• • •

One day there was a violent banging on our front gate. A strange man was flailing a gas can, saying he had run out of gas and needed it filled up. I sent Teddy, our huge fawn-colored Great Dane out of the house and told him to "Sic ' em!" Teddy heard the banging, looked at the gate and promptly walked in the opposite direction. Bruce was in our studio on the property working on the album *You Are Everything* with David Hasselhoff of "Baywatch" fame. Apparently they had finished for the day because David came driving down the driveway from the studio in his black sports car (with the word "KNIGHT" on the plate from his famous TV show "Knight Rider"). The gate automatically opened and the guy with the gas can stopped yelling, pointed at David and said "Hey! You're. . ." David flashed his million-dollar smile at him and said "Yeah, I am" and drove off. We never heard from the guy with the gas can again. I guess he filled up somewhere else.

When they wrapped the project, David did a photoshoot with our dogs and horses. Then they took a video of Bruce driving the big green John Deere tractor with Hasselhoff in the bucket, laughing. What a sight!

• • •

Of course, our boating life carried on but now on a beautiful fifty-five foot Grand Banks Alaskan in the Pacific and harbored at Channel Islands Marina. We hung out there with our boating friends Mickey and Randy as often as we could. The getaway was essential.

Aboard our Pacific Ocean "Odin"

• • •

We had the good fortune of being included in many wonderful parties thanks to Quincy. At the top of the list are his birthday parties. On one occasion this particular party was at Quincy's house. Everyone was there. Bruce and I sat on a couch having a delightful conversation with Gregory Peck and his wife Veronique. They had just returned from a visit to Russia and were telling us how much the Russians loved American jazz.

Michael Jackson was upstairs in Quincy's bedroom and didn't want to come down, but Kidada and I finally convinced him to come down to meet everyone. I think he danced with Dyan Cannon. I know I danced with Emanuel Lewis.

At one party held at Tatou, a lovely restaurant in LA, I danced with Michael Caine. He and Quincy were born on the same day and the same year. Some of the guests at this party included Elizabeth Taylor, Oprah Winfrey, Michael Caine's wife Shakira, George Michael, Ray Charles, Sidney Poitier, Barbra Streisand, Mo and Evelyn Ostin, and Don Rickles.

At another birthday party held at Spago, another fabulous LA. restaurant, there was the usual crowd. Stevie Wonder sang "Happy Birthday," Red Buttons told jokes and Oprah gave a birthday tribute to Michael Caine and Quincy. I was sitting next to Harrison Ford and Calista Flockhart, who were so much in love. I told Calista that when Quincy had asked Harrison what type of music he liked, Harrison replied, "Anything that makes me want to rub up against a woman." At one point Naomi Campbell complained that no one wanted to dance with her so I volunteered. Quincy is so special; he always includes all of his ex-wives and girlfriends at these parties. It's great! They all get along!

Another party was held at Mo and Evelyn Ostin's beautiful home on a hilltop in Bel Air. It was a small group. Elizabeth Taylor was among the guests, as was Lena Horne and Maurice Gibb, who told Bruce, "You look like a British Wing Commander!" Bruce and I had the privilege of being seated at a table with Sidney Poitier and his wife Joanna, plus Miles Davis and Cicely Tyson, along with two of Miles' art dealers. Miles was sitting next to me. He took a cocktail napkin, did a quick sketch of his trumpet lady, wrote down their phone number and handed it to me. I took it home and framed it.

Miles Davis' trumpet lady sketch

• • •

It was around Christmas when Bruce and I were invited to Verna Harrah's house for a lovely dinner. The other guests were Quincy, Peggy, and their girls, who were so cute. Verna had obtained a Santa Claus suit from one of the film studio's costume departments. Bruce was talked into being Santa. He made the best Santa I've ever seen. He was very believable until Kidada said, "Oh, it's just Bruce."

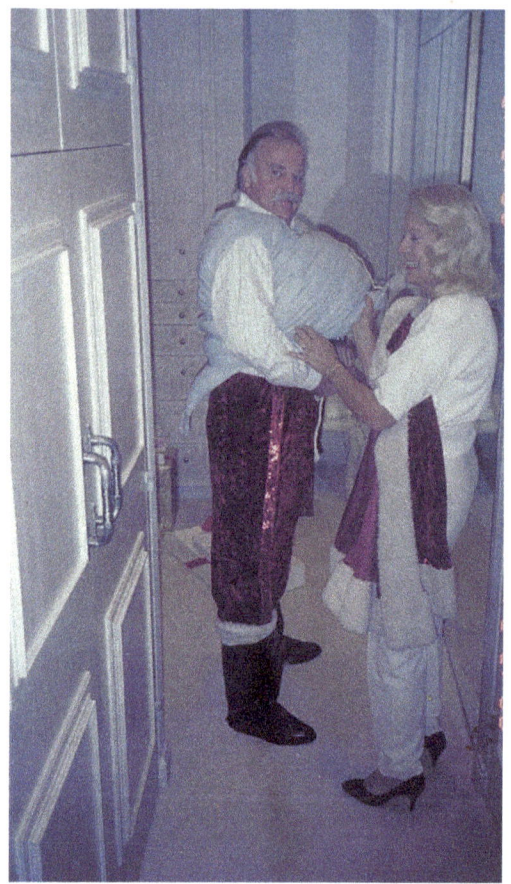

Getting Bruce dressed up as Santa for Quincy's kids

Verna was a film producer and philanthropist, the widow of casino magnate Bill Harrah. She gave the most incredible parties. At one party I was in heaven as we were served Beluga caviar in a huge bowl. My weakness is caviar so I was in hog heaven. This party was with a Latin flair; the guests included Paul Simon, songwriter Sammy Cahn, romance novel writer Jackie Collins, Carrie Fisher, Whoopi Goldberg, Robert De Niro, and of course Quincy, Verna's love. This was after Quincy and Peggy had divorced. Verna and Quincy dated for a few years. She adored him beyond belief. It was so sad when Verna died from cancer. All that money couldn't buy her more time on earth.

• • •

1982 was a busy year. Bruce recorded Donna Summer's big hit "State of Independence" with Quincy. There's a terrific video on YouTube of the backup vocal session. The singers were Lionel Richie, Michael Jackson, Dionne Warwick, James Ingram, Kenny Loggins, Patti Austin, Dyan Cannon, Christopher Cross, Michael McDonald, Brenda Russell, Peggy Lipton, and Stevie Wonder. Only Quincy could get that stellar bunch to sing backup!

Bruce also worked on Ron Howard's movie *Night Shift* that year, which starred Henry Winkler and Michael Keaton. There was music by Rufus and Chaka Khan, as well as The Pointer Sisters, and a lot of the tracks were composed by Burt Bacharach and Carole Bayer Sager. They also composed for the Roberta Flack album *I'm the One* that Bruce recorded that year.

Another album was *E.T.-The Extra-Terrestrial* from the smash hit movie by Steven Spielberg. It was narrated by Michael and produced by Quincy, with music by John Williams. Rod wrote the beautiful song "Someone in the Dark" with lyrics by Alan and Marilyn Bergman. Michael and Quincy won a Grammy for it. They were all so happy to do this project. Michael loved the story and the character. But the record company executives pulled the album from the record stores because they didn't want it to compete with Michael's upcoming release.

But there was to be one more project that year…

• • •

Thriller sold a million copies a month in the U.S. alone. It was made in just eight weeks. And it's the best-selling album of all time. Michael was adamant that it be more than just an album of music. He wanted to show that *Off the Wall* wasn't a fluke. He wanted to make a statement.

Bruce and Quincy were right there with him. They decided before they started that *Thriller* was going to be an event. Michael would often write songs in his head and either sing them, track by track—beatboxing the drums, then turning his voice into a guitar or bass or synthesizer— or hire musicians to cut a demo in his home studio. He brought in several great tunes this way, including the immortal "Billie Jean." To write the rest of the album, Quincy called in a diverse roster, including David Paich and Steve Lukather from the band Toto ("Human Nature"), and of course Rod Temperton, who wrote "Baby Be Mine" and "The Lady in My Life." Rod also came in with a little song called "Starlight." It was a good pop song, but once everyone saw how strong the other material was, they knew "Starlight" wasn't good enough. Rod said he went to sleep wondering what to do and woke up with the word "thriller" in his head. Using the same backing music, he rewrote the lyrics, and the album now had its beating heart, as well as its title.

Bruce wanted Max the dog to do the wolf howls for the intro. He bribed him with hamburgers and even took him out by the barn to listen to the coyotes at night, but Max wasn't interested. Michael ended up doing those wolf howls himself.

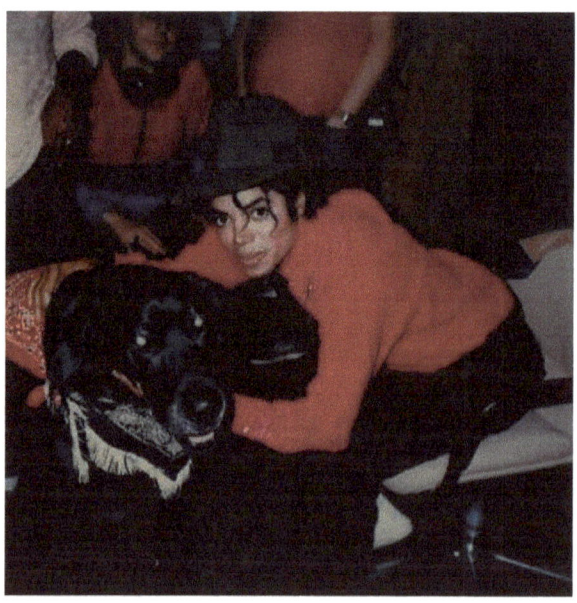

Michael and Max—studio friends

Bruce had a strong memory of the Vincent Price rap session, writing: *"Quincy's wife, Peggy Lipton, knew Vincent Price. So Quincy and Peggy got together and called him. Vincent said he would love to do it.*

Rod's idea, at first, was that Vincent would just talk some horror talk from the type of lines he had delivered in some of his famous roles.

The night before the session with Vincent Price, I remember Quincy and Rod on the phone, talking excitedly about something to do with Vincent's part in "Thriller."

I was getting the tape ready for Vincent to overdub on, so I only overheard bits and pieces of Quincy and Rod's conversation. At about noon, Quincy shows up at the studio, looking like the 'cat that swallowed the canary.' Q looked at me and said, "Svensk, Vincent Price is going to be here at 2 PM. Rod is writing Vincent's rap lyrics in the taxicab on the way here to the studio."

Quincy told me, "I don't think that Vincent has ever been on a pop record before. This should be interesting." And it was more than just interesting. I get chills just thinking about it.

The next thing I knew, Rod came roaring into the control room with several sheets of paper in one hand and a Marlboro cigarette in his mouth, with a two-inch ash ready to fall on the floor. Out of breath, Roddy said to me, "Bruce, quick. . . he's here! I saw a car pull up, and it was Vincent Price. He's on his way in!" He thrust the papers in my hand and said, "Give these to the secretary and have her photocopy these quick!"

Once this was done, we put the 'Rap' lyrics on the music stand. Vincent walked in, sat down on his chair, off he went, and it was all done in about two hours. Vincent Price had never used earphones in his work before. He reluctantly put them on, and when the music track for "Thriller" started, he jumped up from his stool with a startled look on his face. I know he had never heard anything like that before."

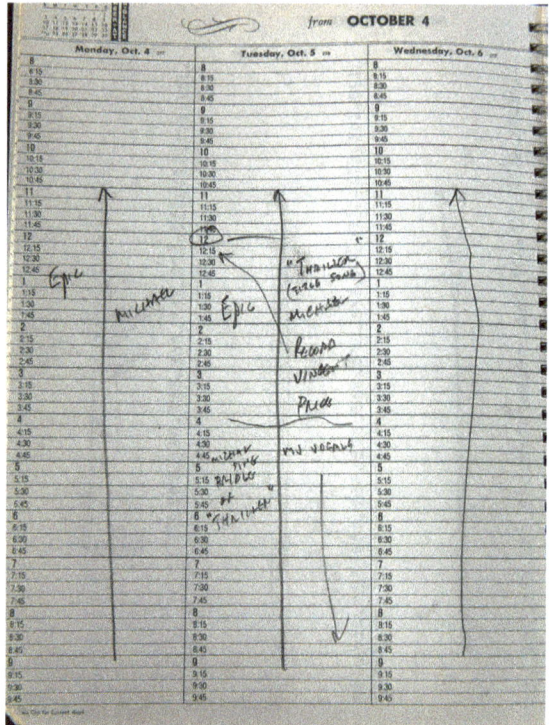

Bruce's datebook from "Thriller."
At noon on October 5th, 1982 they recorded Vincent Price's famous rap.

• • •

Michael also worked with Eddie Van Halen and Paul McCartney. Even though I was used to seeing huge stars, it was extra exciting to hang out with a Beatle. Michael and Paul got along so well together, they decided to keep going after recording "The Girl Is Mine" for *Thriller*, and they ended up creating several more songs together.

When Quincy decided to get Eddie Van Halen to play the guitar solo on "Beat It," he called Eddie, who, when Quincy said "Hi, this is Quincy Jones," said, "F You!" and slammed down the phone, thinking it was a prank call. It took Quincy a few more times before Eddie realized it really was Quincy Jones on the other end of the line. On the track, just before Eddie Van Halen's guitar solo, a noise can be heard that sounds like somebody knocking on a door. It was rumored that the knock was someone entering the recording studio. However, that sound was just Michael knocking on a drum case. He is credited in the liner notes as the "drum case beater."

Bruce didn't record Eddie's guitar solo because he was worried that the decibels might damage his hearing. "*It was so loud I would never subject my hearing to that kind of volume level,*" he later wrote. "*I didn't record that solo, I hired his engineer. I figured his hearing would probably be a little suspect right now anyway. I then did the mix after it was recorded.*"

Meanwhile, to get the sounds Michael and Quincy wanted, Bruce had to invent new ways of recording. For "Billie Jean," Quincy told Bruce to create a drum sound no one had ever heard before. So Bruce built a special drum platform and a flat piece of wood to put between the snare and hi-hat, but still the sound wasn't quite right. They wanted something tighter in the low end, something that would compel people to dance. That's when Bruce made the famous bass drum cover, which he used to get a super isolated sound. He also mixed the song 91 times, until it was just right. Other inventions included a platform for Michael to stand on while he sang, and having Michael sing his backing vocals at different distances from the microphone to create a natural reverb effect. Quincy had the wide angle view of the project and Michael was the talent, but Bruce was the wizard figuring out how to create the sounds. He was a creative partner.

Matt Forger was the second engineer on *Thriller* and many other projects with Bruce, Michael, and Quincy. He remembers, "There has to be a captain to steer the ship, make decisions and chart the course, and that was Bruce. His commanding demeanor and calm attitude always kept the situation under control. He had a steady hand on the rudder, keeping an even keel, guiding us on the journey. He would read Quincy's intent, even if it wasn't apparent to others, and then Q would remark 'That's it, Svensk.' If there was tension in the air he would break the ice with a humorous remark that would relax everyone. A good laugh, and then back to work. The highest compliment I can recall was in a conversation I had with Ed Cherney who preceded me in assisting for Quincy and Bruce. After he left his position at Westlake Studios he went out on his own as an independent engineer and he was engineering for some significant artists and working with big name producers. Eddie said to me, 'When I get into a difficult situation, I think to myself. What would Bruce do?'"

Bruce always said that if it was up to him he'd still be mixing the bass intro on "Billie Jean." He was such a fanatic about every aspect of the sound and the music. Once, when Bruce was mixing "Beat It" at Westlake Studios, something especially memorable happened. I'll let Bruce tell the story:

"During my mix, the speaker actually caught fire and was engulfed in flames! We had to call the techs in and they put the fire out with fire extinguishers. Michael loved that and he has always said that my mix was so hot that it caused the speaker to catch fire! I don't think so. It's a nice thought, though…"

They found out later it was just a short-circuit in an amplifier.

The "Beat It" speaker after the fire

• • •

When it came time to finish *Thriller*, Bruce, Quincy, Michael, Rod and Matt worked nonstop. There was a snag before the release.

Bruce later talked about it with writer Marsha Vdovin in an interview for Bill Putnam, Jr.'s recording equipment company Universal Audio:

"The guys from Epic thought they were taking Thriller *home with them, the release. But we took it back. . . . Throughout [the] recording, I'd been telling everyone in the studio, 'There's just too much time per side on the album.' At that point in time, we were doing LPs, of course. Because of the groove width and spacing and so on, that controls the quality. Or, the amount of low end material that can fit greatly affects the quality of sound we can carve onto it. CDs are so simple, there's nothing to it. But back when we were making LPs, that was a whole other thing.*

"So I got the master disc back from Bernie Grundman's, and we're in the control room at Westlake. Michael, Quincy, Rod Temperton, and I were all listening intensely. When we were almost halfway through, we noticed that Michael had snuck out of the control room, and went across the hall to Studio B. I went over there to check on him. Michael's in the corner, sobbing… just sobbing his heart out. Because, well, the sound quality wasn't very good. There was way too much material on the record—it was way, way over time. In those days of the LP, the quality and the low end that you could get out of a record was directly influenced by the length of the music. Now, the guys from Epic thought they were taking Thriller *home with them, the release. But we took it back. Quincy said, 'No, you're not getting this record right now. It isn't done.' Then he sent the guys from Epic home. Ooooh man, were they pissed! So Quincy did some fast editing. He cut time everywhere that he could, so that we could get the sides down to where I could get some real level on the master. Then we gave it back to them. You know, I don't think that many people know that story."*

Universal Audio actually sells a plug-in that models the very Harrison 32C console that Bruce recorded *Thriller* on. It is very popular.

· · ·

Michael had seen the horror film *An American Werewolf in London* and wanted the director John Landis to do the *Thriller* short film—Michael never called it a music video. Bruce fit the music to the visual. It only took four days to film and cost half a million dollars, the most expensive ever at the time. There were forty make-up artists turning dancers into undead zombies. The choreography was fantastic and the dance continues to be performed all over the world.

There was a panic before the release. Michael, at the time a Jehovah's Witness, was told there would be repercussions if he released the film, so he inserted a disclaimer at the beginning: "Due to my strong personal convictions, I wish to stress that this film in no way endorses a belief in the occult."

We were invited to the private premiere at a theater in West Hollywood. Eddie Murphy, Diana Ross, and Prince were there. The place was crawling with fans and the press. It was like a major motion picture premiere! Michael watched it from the projection booth. It received a standing ovation and they played it twice. Then, of course, it debuted on MTV and the rest is history. Music videos were changed forever.

Ready for the Grammys!

*"To Bea, Thanks for taking care of
Bruce your sweet Love, Michael Jackson"*

Bruce's work on *Thriller* won him his first Grammy Award for Best Engineered Album, Non-Classical in 1984. It was so exciting! Going to the Grammys was ridiculous fun. You think it's all happening at night, but it's not. The pre-ceremony, where they announce many of the winners, was at 12:30 in the afternoon. So we were dressed to the nines, Bruce wearing one of his lucky ties, in our stretch limo, heading out from our ranch to the Shrine Auditorium in downtown LA at 10 in the morning. (I still have a closet full of all my "Grammy Gowns.") Once we arrived, there were flashbulbs everywhere. Of course, this was the *Thriller* Grammys—twelve nominations and eight wins. The people, the press, the limos, the glamor and glitz, posing for pictures on the red carpet—all of it was unforgettable, including seeing our studio friends all dressed up for a change.

Working on *Thriller* was a phenomenal project in the studio, but when you are suddenly a part of the publicity and recognition, that was something completely different. Our seats were close to the front because Bruce was a part of that stellar team. The ceremony and live performances were electric. It was long too. When I needed to go and powder my nose, the minute I left my seat, a glamorously dressed person (called a "seat filler") quickly sat in my place until I came back, so the cameras never showed an empty seat in the audience. After the ceremony came the after-parties, which were always spectacular. Each record label would host a star-studded party with the best of everything. Table-hopping was always fun and it was especially nice since we were acquainted with most everyone. And there was a lot of schmoozing. New deals were often started at those Grammy parties.

• • •

Michael, Bruce, our ranch hand Julio Juarez
and family, and Max at our home

This picture was taken in the mid-'80s, by which point Michael was the most famous man on the planet.

Not a lot of people got to see him like this, just hanging out. He was very quiet, but, as I said, he had a subtle sense of humor. He was very sincere. The success of *Thriller* didn't seem to change him. He was always the same with Bruce, me, Quincy, and the gang. We were like family. When we'd spend the weekend at Neverland, we'd all get in our pajamas and watch movies in bed. He didn't drink, he didn't do drugs, he didn't swear.

Quincy once said that he and Michael had sort of a father/son relationship, with love and respect for each other. He described Michael as being "very grounded, very spiritual, very focused, very courteous and kind. He never threw his weight around and was fun to be with. We saw him grow as an artist."

But being constantly followed and harassed by paparazzi, and being dragged through the mud on a regular basis in the tabloids (which often seeped into the broader news cycles of the industry) took a toll on him.

The only way he could go into the world as a normal person was in disguise. He had unbelievable makeup and prosthetics. His favorite alter ego was a Jewish man named Mr. Sherman. He had a hideout in Beverly Hills with a doorman at the gate—a little two-bedroom place on the second floor. Ronald and Nancy Reagan had a condo there.

On many occasions I would drive Michael home to his hideout. When we would pull up to the security gate he would get in the back seat of Bruce's Bronco and lie down so as to not be seen by the guard. He told me that the security guard would notify many of his fans that Michael was there and pretty soon there would be a crowd of them outside the gate. On entering we would pull into his first floor garage and take the elevator to his apartment. He was always so gracious and kind to Bruce and me. One time I was in his game room when he said, "Just a minute, I'll be right back" and disappeared. All of a sudden, an old man with a white beard was standing behind me. I was terrified, until the old man said in that familiar soft voice, "Don't worry, Bea, it's me." The disguise worked!

Occasionally on a Sunday Bruce and Michael would go to the studio just to listen to what they had been working on. They would then drive out to our ranch in Moorpark. We would all pile into our golf cart and drive through the orange groves across the street. One Sunday while on our tour of the groves we met up with a daughter of Julio Juarez, who worked there. She was so shocked to see Michael she couldn't speak. But Michael soon put her at ease and they talked for a while. Soon after, Julio and his kids showed up at our ranch with two huge crates of oranges for Michael. When we drove Michael back to the apartment in Westwood where he was staying, he shared some of the oranges with the doorman.

• • •

Trumpeter Herb Alpert was an old friend. He was famous for his band The Tijuana Brass in the '60s and for co-founding A&M Records around the same time. Bruce loved that studio and really loved the fact that it was built on the 1918 Charlie Chaplin movie lot. He worked with Herb on his album *Blow Your Own Horn* in 1983. Bruce mixed the *Sérgio Mendes* album that same year. It was their first project together and had the hit song "Never Gonna Let You Go," sung by Joe Pizullo. That version became a big hit, peaking at #4 on the Billboard Hot 100. The next year he did Sérgio's album *Confetti*. It was the beginning of a beautiful friendship with Sérgio and his wife Gracinha that still goes on today. Then it was on to Roberta Flack and Peabo Bryson's duet album *Born to Love*. Busy guy! All of it was the best of the best; talent at the highest level. It didn't get any better than what Bruce was doing in those years.

I was busy at home running the business for Bruce's work on all these projects, and I was running the ranch: animals, garden, and fruit trees included. We often had guests who would come and visit, including family and friends from Sweden. Our friend and assistant Judy Kelley helped by taking them sightseeing. They'd go to Universal Studios, Disneyland, or whatever studio Bruce was working in at the time. We shared our fun with them.

• • •

After *Thriller,* the Jackson 5 prepared for their last hurrah, the *Victory* album and tour.

At the time Bruce was briefly back in New York, so when Michael wanted to record a duet with Mick Jagger, the session was scheduled to be at New York's A&R Studios. I went to the studio the morning of the session. Pretty soon I heard them vocalizing in one of the studios. Michael had Mick doing his vocal warm-ups, which were considerable and went on for fifteen minutes non-stop. Just imagine that combo singing scales! Mick was sweet. We sat drinking tea and he was all excited because he and his wife were expecting a baby. Michael's brothers sang backup. He and Michael ended up creating the song "State of Shock."

At lunchtime Bruce was craving White Castle hamburgers, aka "sliders." So one of the security guys and I drove over to Queens and got fifty—yes, fifty—sliders. Mick loved them. However, Michael called them "mouseburgers" and declined the offer to try one. When we were back home in LA we were listening to the radio and couldn't believe that the DJ played "State of Shock," which Michael and Mick had recorded for the Jacksons album, non-stop for twenty-four hours. About a week later, when I was back in California, I was out in our horse barn when the phone rang. It was Mick calling from his home in the Caribbean. I told him about the crazy DJ. His only comment was, "How boring!" I told him the DJ said he figured Michael and Mick needed the money.

Bruce, me, Mick Jagger and Michael during the "State of Shock" sessions

• • •

Around this time, Michael recorded "Say, Say, Say" with Paul McCartney in London. While they were filming the video for that song near Los Olivos, California, Michael fell in love with the Sycamore Valley Ranch and said he wanted it to be his someday. In 1988 he bought the 2,700-acre property and named it Neverland Ranch.

Michael and I shared a deep love for animals. He had always had pets since he was a kid and loved hearing my stories about India and was so curious about our life there. He was always asking questions about it. My best friend in the Naga Hills was a chicken named Easy because he was so easy to catch. Unfortunately, one day Shiloh, the cook, caught him and there he was on a platter for dinner that night. Michael always thought that was so sad. Me too.

• • •

Neverland was a refuge Michael created for himself, away from the glitz and hustle of the outside world. It had a huge English country house, a zoo, carnival rides, a movie theater, and a huge lake. He had many animals there, amongst them tigers, Gypsy the elephant, a giraffe, deer, a lion, a llama named Louie, and a huge boa constrictor named Muscles who he would frequently bring to the studio.

One morning I drove up to the Neverland gate and was stopped by a couple of Secret Service guys who proceeded to sweep underneath my Suburban with mirrors, looking for explosive devices. It turned out that Nancy Reagan was coming to visit Michael later that day.

Bruce and I got Michael a beautiful white canoe for paddling around the lakes on the ranch. No motors or engines on a canoe! Blissfully quiet. Michael loved the water. Swimming and boating were favorite pastimes. We drove the hundred miles from Moorpark to Neverland in our Suburban, canoe sticking out the back. Little did the people on the road know who that boat was for.

The canoe we got for Michael

• • •

We decided to take several months off to do some traveling and since Bruce had never been there, we planned to go to Sweden to meet our extended families. The day before we were to leave, passports in hand, luggage packed, and Judy settled in to take care of all of our animals, the phone rang. It was Herb Alpert. He wanted Bruce to mix the theme song "All Time High" for the movie *Octopussy*, which had been recorded by Rita Coolidge. "Sorry, Herb," I heard Bruce say on the phone, "can't do it 'cause we're leaving for Sweden." Silence… then I heard Bruce say, "OK, we'll change our plans and I'll kill the mix." When Bruce got off the phone he looked at me and said, "Honey, he's made me an offer I can't refuse." Going with the flow as always, I made a few phone calls and changed our schedule. Eventually we did get to Sweden after all, where we visited the beautiful town of Stöde, where there have been Swediens—originally spelled Svedin—since 1625. Bruce's cousin Per Lindstrom was married to the actress Ingrid Bergman in the town's beautiful little church, and years later Roberta played concerts there in front of an audience full of newfound relatives. After our trip to Sweden we came back to California, where a horse of ours was in a horse show in Santa Barbara. We spent the rest of our time off cruising the California coast on the boat.

By this time we had a 70-foot trawler built by the Norwegian Romsdal Shipbuilders. We traveled all the way to the west coast of Norway to find that ultimate *Odin*, which had a fireplace and slept twelve people. The previous owner sailed it to us through the Panama Canal, into the Pacific and up to Los Angeles. It was the ultimate getaway and Bruce and I could handle it in and out of port by ourselves.

Our little ship "Odin"

• • •

Michael was filming a commercial for Pepsi in January of 1984 to the music of "Beat It" when the pyrotechnics went off too early and part of his hair caught on fire and was burned off down to his scalp! Safety standards back then were not at all what they are now. There was no firefighting equipment and all the crew could do was put the flames out with their hands. Michael was rushed by ambulance with second- and third-degree burns to his face and scalp. It was horrible. He was prescribed opiates for the pain, which started a dependence on drugs that would be a problem for the rest of his life. We all felt so sorry for him.

• • •

Shortly after that, the new wave band Missing Persons asked Bruce to produce their album *Rhyme and Reason*. Peter Max would do their video. Chuck Wild was the keyboard player and he has been another longtime, dear friend. He is now the musician behind Liquid Mind, the perfect music for relaxation and sleep. The Missing Persons album was recorded at Westlake. Chuck remembers a busy studio. "The band was in the control room with Bruce," he says. "I had just come in laden with food for the troops. Quincy was in the studio, having a meeting about the upcoming movie *The Color Purple* with Oprah, and Sidney Poitier was soon going to be coming in to visit. And Michael was practicing his dance steps right outside the control room door! It was a buzz of energy that I will never forget. Super-charged work and creative fun all at the same time."

It was because of this commitment to the Missing Persons project that Bruce had to turn Quincy down for the "We Are The World" session. Quincy was not at all happy about this. It was an amazing project that Quincy and Lionel Richie and Michael put together. Quincy could move the earth. And he did so, many, many times. "We Are The World" was incredible.

• • •

The 1985 film *The Color Purple* was an adaptation of Alice Walker's best-selling book. Quincy was an integral part of the creation of this groundbreaking film about one African-American woman's struggles in the American south. Steven Spielberg directed, Quincy produced, composed and arranged the music and Bruce recorded and mixed it. The movie was nominated for eleven Academy Awards, including Best Picture, Best Music, Original Song, and Best Music, Original Score. A lot of the gang played on this album—Quincy's "posse." As with all of

Bruce's film work, we were almost never on the set. It was all done in the studio.

That summer Bruce was set to give a lecture in Stockholm. Our old friend Bjorn Asplind had arranged a surprise: "I asked Bruce and Bea to come to Gothenburg four days early," he explains. "I had tickets for all of us to go on the Göta Canal trip. You go from Gothenburg to Stockholm on a boat that goes through lakes and canals all the way up to Stockholm. The trip takes fours days and you pass through 58 locks. To Bruce's delight there was fantastic food on the boat. We met up with our friends Leif and Margareta Allansson in Stockholm and then traveled around Sweden visitng friends and family. We had such a fabulous time on that trip connecting to our Swedish roots."

The next year, Bruce produced, recorded, and mixed the music for the Chicago action comedy movie *Running Scared* starring Billy Crystal and Gregory Hines. Rod composed the music and a lot of our old pals were on the project: Siedah, Jerry Hey, Greg Phillinganes, and all. Michael McDonald sang Rod's song "Sweet Freedom" on that film and it went on to be a Top 10 Hit on the Billboard Chart.

Around this time Bruce did an album with saxophonist, keyboard player and composer Edgar Winter. When they were in the studio his wife Monique would take me shopping on Rodeo Drive. Not my usual haunt by any means, but we had great fun!

· · ·

By the time the Jacksons' tour ended, *Thriller* had sold twenty million copies, and the anticipation for Michael's next album grew to a feverish pitch. To ease the tension, Quincy suggested Michael begin working on his next solo project, which would become *Bad*. We knew each other so well now, the sessions were more like a family reunion. Every Friday night, Michael's cooks, "The Slam Dunk Sisters," would make a whole buffet. Anyone could come eat, including all the session musicians and their friends. I remember one night we had an extra special guest: Michael brought Muscles, a huge python in a container.

By now, anything to do with Michael was a whirlwind. He had reached an unprecedented level of stardom. The pressure was immense, but so was the bond among Michael, Quincy, and Bruce. Bruce and Quincy worked in the studio around the clock. Quincy once joked that they had to carry out the second engineers on stretchers.

On the song "Smooth Criminal," Bruce did the voice of the cop yelling "Okay, I want everybody to clear the area RIGHT NOW!" He walked around the house rehearsing it at the top of his lungs. We wondered what the neighbors thought.

Bruce loved all the songs he did with Michael, but he especially loved this album. I met Siedah Garrett, who composed the lyrics to "Man in the Mirror," at the *Bad* sessions and we have been friends ever since. What a talent! Siedah also co-wrote "Keep the Faith" on the *Dangerous* album, as well as many other songs. She brings an energy to every project she works on. She has a terrific sense of humor, is always knitting something fabulous and tells it like it is. She has a voice that doesn't quit and she is true blue.

About the experience, Bruce later wrote: *"As far as I'm concerned, the song 'Man In The Mirror,' composed by Glen Ballard and Siedah Garrett, is the centerpiece, musically speaking, of the Michael Jackson album* Bad.

I recorded the Andraé Crouch choir on 'Man In The Mirror' with only two microphones. I used my favorite pair of Neumann M-49s in the classic Blumlein Pair method. One of my unquestionably favorite true, stereophonic microphone techniques, this is perhaps the best known of all single-point stereo microphone techniques.

What is the effect on the choir in 'Man In The Mirror'? In my lectures and seminars, around the world, I have often been asked [that question]. Isn't that something? There is no effect on the choir on 'Man In The Mirror.' Or very, very little!

I try to explain by saying that the recording of the choir on 'Man In The Mirror' is a classic but simple stereo microphone technique. Of course, in addition, you have the best gospel choir in the world, in one of the best studios in the world: Westlake Audio's gorgeous Studio D in Hollywood.

This wonderful piece of music has a graceful, natural-sounding dynamic curve to it. From the transparent, burnished brass synthesized bells in the intro to the Andraé Crouch choir that comes in at the modulation and, of course, the music climaxes with the huge ending."

No sooner had they completed the album than they were shooting the videos. The video for the song "Bad" was shot on location in a subway station in New York and was directed by Martin Scorsese.

When Michael filmed the video for "Smooth Criminal," we, along with Carina, a cousin of mine from Sweden, went to sit in. During a break Michael, dressed in the gorgeous white suit he wore for the shoot, came out of his dressing room carrying Bubbles, who was, thank God, not fully grown yet. He put the little chimp in Carina's lap where the rascal promptly unbuttoned her blouse. Bruce yelled, "Michael, you've trained him well."

Mark Hagen, a young guy from North Dakota, was interning with Bruce on *Bad*. He remembers: *"During the* Bad *album project I was very inexperienced, but to me Michael seemed really focused, healthy, and in top form with his voice. In the 35 years since, I've worked with so many great singers, but none better than Michael. R.I.P. What an amazing unparalleled talent and to me a genuine guy, yet he was such a shy, insecure, complicated person too. One night I was doing my studio runner duties and vacuuming upstairs at Westlake when Bruce approached me and said, 'Mark, would you give Michael a ride home?' Evidently MJ was dropped off at the studio and someone showed up at his parents' house for a scheduled meeting that Michael had forgotten about. I wish I would've gotten a Polaroid picture of that: Michael riding along wearing a surgical mask and a fedora in my blue '77 Honda Civic with a rusty roof. We made small talk the entire way to Encino and I could tell it was a great adventure for Michael. When we pulled up to the gate on Hayvenhurst, per usual there were about 20 fans hanging out to catch a glimpse, yet nobody paid any attention to my car until he was up to the gate and they noticed who my passenger was."*

One day we were in a studio in New York where Bruce and Mr. Scorsese were mixing the song to picture. I was relaxing in the 'green room' and was shocked to see a really large rat run across the room and disappear under a couch. Only in New York! After the work in New York was completed, we all flew back to LA on the Sony Jet, just in time for Thanksgiving.

• • •

We went on the "Bad" tour to Japan with Michael and Quincy and the gang. This was Michael's first tour as a solo artist. It was a very big deal for everyone.

Before we left, Bruce and I joined Michael and all the musicians and dancers for rehearsals at an indoor arena in Pensacola, Florida. The sound truck was driven from Los Angeles. It was the same crew that had worked with us on Lena Horne's Broadway show. During one of the rehearsals in this large, empty basketball arena, I found a folding chair and placed it in the center of the basketball court. It was incredible to be the only member of the audience. When the rehearsal was over I yelled and applauded. Michael yelled back, "That's gotta be Bea!"

We had a jumbo jet just for the crew, which included Bruce, me, Quincy, his son Quincy III (aka Snoopy), Michael, Mark Ross, son of Time Warner CEO Steve Ross, and his wife Sally, music lover and Harvard professor Jerold Kayden, keyboardist Greg Phillinganes, all the musicians, Miko Brando, Michael's two chefs, and of course Bubbles the chimp. While we were still in LAX airport, in a very secure VIP lounge, in came Marlon Brando. He was there to say goodbye to his son Miko, who did security and was a good friend of Michael's. Marlon looked over at me and slowly licked his lips.

When we arrived in Tokyo, half of the Narita airport had been closed for our security. However, 1,500 passes had been issued to the international press. What chaos as these photographers swarmed around us! We were alongside Michael and the security guards told us to make a circle around Michael. Of course, we were very aware of Michael's incredible fame, but we were used to being with him in the studio, where he would walk in just like anyone else. We hadn't expected this. The energy and excitement were insane.

Quincy, Michael and Bruce in Tokyo on the "Bad" tour

Bubble's trainer, Bubbles and me

Michael was just himself with us. Quiet, sweet, and polite. He was busy with rehearsals and press conferences. We had a few floors of the hotel and all hung out together, Bubbles included. We were like a family.

One evening Quincy, Christine, Snoopy, Mark and Sally, Jerold, Bruce and I were invited to dinner at a lovely restaurant by Akio Morita, who was the co-founder of Sony. While chatting at dinner, he wanted to know more about each of us so he asked about our background.

Later that week we realized why he had been curious about our heritage. It was for the dinner menu! We were all invited to his home where two chefs from the Japanese imperial palace had prepared dinner. There was (of course) Kobe beef for the guys, pizza for Quincy Jr., and what a shock for me to be served Indian curry! The Moritas were such a lovely couple. Michael became lifelong friends with them. When Mr. Morita had a stroke in 1993 Michael made a tape of healing music and words for him to listen to every day.

Before every one of Michael's concerts we were picked up at the hotel in a large bus and transported to the theater. Backstage, there were huge food stalls. The shows were spectacular and we were surprised to see how reserved the audience was. Afterwards there would be a reception. Several aspiring American models managed to sneak in to meet Michael and hopefully get their pictures in the press.

We have home movies of everyone hanging out at the hotel. Michael brought Bubbles in. He ran around and amused everyone. We were all used to him since he was in the studio so often. Bubbles was particularly fond of me and jumped in my lap at one point and put his arms around me. I was fine with it, being the animal person I was and having grown up in the jungles of India. But some people were concerned and pulled him off me. Bubbles was growing up and his strength and aggression were starting to be a bit of a problem. Eventually, years later, he lived at the Center for Great Apes in Florida.

Shopping with Quincy and our little group was something I really enjoyed. We went into a huge department store and I led everyone to the fine china area. Beautiful dishes for my dinner parties were my passion. The gang meandered around. Bruce walked in and said to me, "So, did you buy the store?" I did buy a set and had them shipped to LA. The story that the plates my dinner guests were eating from were bought in Tokyo on Michael Jackson's "Bad" tour made for some entertaining table talk.

One night we were invited to a Geisha house by some of the Japanese promoters. Snoopy (Quincy Jr.) was breakdancing and Bruce and Quincy, after a fair amount of sake, sang the song "Sunny" to karaoke. What a cozy bunch we were! On one occasion, Tats, a friend of Quincy's and a nephew to the Emperor, took us to an old Japanese restaurant where we sat on the floor and cooked duck in a pot of hot oil. The owner of the restaurant was an elderly Japanese man. He spoke no English, but after dinner he was weeping. Tats explained to us that he was grateful that our country had dropped the A-bomb as it had saved his life. Apparently he was a kamikaze pilot and would have perished on his mission.

After several days in Tokyo, Bruce and I decided to take the Bullet Train to the town of Mishima, not far from Mt. Fuji. There was an old Swedish cruise ship docked there and it was now a hotel. We had a lovely suite onboard and enjoyed a delicious Swedish dinner. Only one person who worked there spoke any English, but he was so sweet and took us for a ride in a small boat to show us their fish farming.

After we returned from Japan and the "Bad" tour, we were invited to Mark and Sally Ross's wedding in New York. Mark was working for Quincy Jones Productions at the time. The ceremony was conducted on the top deck of a large party boat. As the boat cruised the beautiful New York harbor and around the Statue of Liberty we were alarmed by all of the press photographers in helicopters over our boat. It was a star-studded evening—guests included Barbra Streisand, Steve Ross (the father of the groom and founder of Time Warner), Verna Harrah and Quincy. Since Sally was Episcopalian and Mark was Jewish, the service was performed by both a priest and a rabbi.

While chatting with Sally's father, he mentioned that he often went to India and had heard that was where I grew up. Come to find out he was a friend of Fred and Jane Downs, a couple of missionary kids that we had grown up with in India and gone to school with at Woodstock! Fred was in the same class at Woodstock as my brother Bruce. Small world. But Woodstock alumni could be found everywhere. Once on a flight from New York to Stockholm, the man I was seated next to and I started talking. He had gone to Woodstock too.

• • •

The 1988 Grammys were again held in New York at Radio City Music Hall. There were Grammy billboards all over Manhattan. Of course, nothing could ever compare to *Thriller*, but *Bad* was nominated for six Grammys and Bruce won for Best Engineered Recording, Non-Classical. In addition, "Leave Me Alone" won for Best Video. People were surprised that there weren't more wins because sales were through the roof. Michael performed the next night in his first ever solo concert in New York City at Madison Square Garden. It was insane. Packed to the hilt!

Michael sent us four eight-hundred dollar bottles of champagne, which we enjoyed with Mickey and Randy at the marina while watching the Grammy broadcast they had taped. "Michael liked talking to Mickey on the phone about all the sailing we had done because he had just read the book *Dove* about a young guy who sailed around the world alone," Randy remembers.

• • •

Quincy and Michael Caine shared the same birthday; same day, same year: March 14, 1933. Every year they would celebrate together with a serious, star-studded party. Their sixtieth party was at Tatou in Los Angeles and everyone was there: Elizabeth Taylor, Ray Charles, Sidney Poitier, Jack Nicholson, Oprah, Don Rickles, George Michael, LL Cool J, and of course all of Quincy's kids: Kidada, Rashida, Jolie, Snoopy, and Tina.

I'll never forget standing next to Bruce that night when Barbra Streisand walked in. She saw Bruce and just lit up, a beaming smile spreading across her face as she walked toward him. A few years earlier they had worked together on her album *Till I Loved You*. She loved him. Great musicians always did. He was always there for their music and their artistry. He loved her too. Quincy produced and Bruce recorded and mixed the song "The Places You'll Find Love," with back-up vocals by Dionne Warwick, The Pointer Sisters, Siedah Garrett, James Ingram, Jennifer Holiday, and Luther Vandross. What a backup group!

• • •

The next album up, *Back on the Block*, was a Quincy reunion party and old-home week for Bruce too. Talk about a gang of all-stars: Ella Fitzgerald, Sarah Vaughan, Miles Davis, Dizzy Gillespie, Ray Charles, Luther Vandross, Barry White, George Benson, Take Six, Chaka Khan,

Dionne Warwick, Bobby McFerrin, Al Jarreau, James Ingram, Joe Zawinul, Ice-T, and Quincy Jones III all made appearances on the album. Everyone was in seventh heaven.

Bruce later wrote about the project:

"When Quincy Jones and I, together with Rod Temperton, set out, in March of 1988, to make Quincy's album Back On The Block*, our goal was to make music to take to the streets, to make love to, to reflect upon, to find hope in and to get lost in. Some of the ingredients we used are; the tradition of the African Griot storyteller that we know today as Rap; the sensuous harmonies within Brazilian music; some Be-bop with a dash of hip-hop; the power of a gospel choir; the lush vocals of a Zulu chant; a taste of jazz and an acapella celebration.*

Back On The Block *is another Quincy Jones cast of characters in one piece of music. Combining all the elements involved and yet to be able to retain maximum flexibility was quite a challenge.*

As I have mentioned before, I love a challenge. A piece of music cannot be too complex for me. I am happiest when I am in the studio unraveling some fantastically complicated musical structure.

Well, I almost met my match with this one. For instance, there are twelve independent sets of drums used to realize this piece of music. There are several authentic African instruments, such as the Hinde-Hoo, and the Djembe Bass bass drum. There are actual African drums used for one of the drum sets. Quincy had the lyric translated to Swahili, for the choir, as well.

Both Quincy and I were a bit anxious when it came time to call in the rappers to help conceive, write and perform the verses for this one. We had heard all the stories and read all the bad press. However, we were both very favorably impressed. We asked the rappers to come to the studio on a Wednesday night night to hear our concept, and the scratch track of our ideas and sounds for the track.

The rappers are Ice-T, Big-Daddy Kane, Kool Mo-Dee and Melle-Mel. Not to mention Quincy Jones, and Quincy's son Quincy Jones III.

Quincy sketched some ideas and an outline of the concept for them. We asked them if they could come back Thursday night and we'd see what they had come up with and we would take it further towards completion. They all said, 'We'll be back tomorrow night to RECORD!'

And that's just what they did.

When we decided to do this song, it quickly became evident to me that I would have to have a desk to record and mix it on that was very, very large. Say, at the least, 80 inputs. Most of the large desks available to me at the time would not, in my estimation, give me the huge, open sound that I heard in my mind's ear for this piece of music.

The big desks at that time were full of integrated circuits and as a result the sound of them was, to my ear, constricted and narrow sounding. One morning my old pal Allen Sides, (the man who owns Ocean Way Studios in Hollywood) called, and as we talked, I brought up the idea of doing something Allen and I had talked about for a couple of years. We had both dreamed of having a huge, totally discrete Neve desk of at least 80 inputs. I told Allen that now was the time to do it. Well, we did it!

It is actually two Neve 8078 forty-input desks combined seamlessly into one gigantic, totally discrete desk, with 80 main automated inputs and an additional thirty-two effects returns, making a total of one hundred and twelve inputs. Back On The Block *has many layers and textures that go into the formation of this tone poem of Rap."*

Back on the Block was another massive success. It won seven Grammys, including Album of the Year; Rod Temperton and Jerry Hey won Grammys for their arrangements; and Bruce won a Grammy for Best Engineered Album. They all had a wonderful time making that album, as always. The talent and creativity in one place was incredible… and it was often accompanied by calm, loving, and intense personalities. Quite a combo.

• • •

When Bruce and Michael started making the *Dangerous* album, we all moved into the Hilton Hotel at Universal City to be close to Record One, the studio where they were working. This was Michael's first solo album without Quincy (Bruce co-produced, with Michael, Teddy Riley, and Bill Bottrell). It was time for Michael to spread his wings.

Bruce would go into the studio early every day to set up the session, taking the chauffeured limo to try to fool Michael's fans into thinking that Michael was in the car. That ploy didn't last long. The fans (and paparazzi) eventually discovered that Michael was in the back seat of my Bronco and would shove their cameras literally in his face. He was always gracious about it.

Each day, I would go to Michael's suite and take him down the service elevator, through the kitchen, and out to the car. We chatted on these little trips about family, the weather, animals. He was very curious about my life in India and Nagaland and asked a lot of questions about life and the people there. There was always something interesting to talk about. We felt like old friends.

One morning we got on the elevator and there was a young girl in her hotel uniform. Michael could see that she was shocked to see him. He soon put her at ease by asking her where she worked in the hotel and told her that she was very pretty. The poor girl never said a word but almost passed out! Not long after that, the hotel guests realized that Michael was staying there.

One memorable night Bruce, Michael, and I left the studio at about 3 AM. A car pulled up alongside us at a stoplight and the couple in the car started calling Michael's name. Michael, against our advice, opened the window and talked to them. It seems that when Michael was in the hospital in Santa Monica after he had been burned filming the Pepsi commercial, these two had camped outside the hospital for days. Michael had and still has many loyal fans.

That Halloween evening, I found myself driving Michael back to the hotel in Universal City. The streets were full of little kids trick-or-treating. Michael looked at them wistfully and said he had never been able to go with other kids on Halloween as he and his brothers were usually working in a club somewhere.

Another night—actually it was three in the morning—Bruce, Michael, and I rode back together to our hotel. When we got there, Michael discovered that he had misplaced his room key, so the three of us went to our room where we phoned the front desk to get a replacement key. Michael had registered under the name "Mr. Sherman" so I informed the front desk that we needed to get "Mr. Sherman" to his room. We were told that a night manager would bring up a key. We waited and waited. After about forty-five minutes, I phoned the front desk again. "Someone will be right up," I was told. Again, nothing. While we waited, Bruce, Michael and I chatted about anything and everything. The next time I called the hotel people, I requested that they send up a cot. Finally a man arrived with a key and let poor sleepy Michael into his suite.

• • •

When an album has been completed, the record company executives are typically invited to a playback session at one of the studios where it had been recorded so they can get a sneak preview of the final result. The playback session for *Dangerous* had been arranged by Michael's managers, Jim Morey and Sandy Gallin; it was to be held at Larrabee Studios in Burbank. Up until this time, Michael had refused to attend any of these playback sessions.

We finally convinced Michael to attend this one. When we arrived at the studio there was a lovely buffet lunch provided for all of us by his managers. Michael was hanging out with Macauley Culkin and having a great time goofing off.

We, along with the Sony executives, got seated in Studio A. Bruce and his assistant started playing all the songs from the album: "Remember the Time," "Jam," "Heal the World," and of course the title track "Dangerous." After we had heard all this incredible music, all of the Sony people stood up and walked out of the studio. Not one of them had any comments. Sandy Gallin was furious. I saw him standing in the hall yelling at these fools. "Are you brain dead?" Not one comment from these idiots.

Michael was in tears. "Now you know why I've never gone to a playback session," he said. We got him into our car and tried to console him. He deserved much more than to be treated like that.

The executives were wrong, of course. *Dangerous* went platinum in a month, hit #1 on the Billboard Top Albums chart, was one of the biggest selling albums of the 1990s, and has sold over 32 million copies. Bruce was nominated for two Grammys: as co-composer of "Jam" for Best Rhythm and Blues Song and for Best Engineered Album, Non-Classical, which he won. Michael received the Grammy Legend Award and *Dangerous* had multiple nominations and wins at the American Music Awards and Soul Train Music Awards. It also won Best Worldwide Album at the 1992 Billboard Music Awards.

The "Dangerous" Grammys: Bruce, me and Roberta

A kiss for good luck

And 30,000 albums were stolen from a warehouse at Los Angeles International Airport by armed robbers even before it was released!

Michael's song "Will You Be There?" from *Dangerous* was used in the film *Free Willy*. When Bruce was mixing the track at our studio in Moorpark we got to know Basil Poledouris, who had written much of the score for the film. We became good friends with Basil and his lovely wife Bobbie. Unfortunately, Basil died from lung cancer when he was only 61. He had composed the music for the films *The Blue Lagoon*, *The Hunt for Red October*, *Lonesome Dove* and many others as well. How very sad that we lost him so soon.

• • •

Around this time Bruce and I had an urge for the Florida Keys, so we flew to Miami, rented a car and drove to the islands, stopping at vistas along the way. It felt like heaven to both of us. And what an escape! Bruce loved driving along the Seven Mile Bridge. We bought a house on the waterfront on Ramrod (yes, Ramrod) Key, and later, the two adjoining properties. Bruce also loved snorkeling and would spend hours swimming with the amazing sea life in that clear, blue-green water. The restaurants were fabulous, some of them little more than shacks with the most delicious seafood you could ever eat. We met Charlie and Judi Riggi there, dear friends to this day. There was a raccoon that hung around our beach—we named him Ricky Rack. I took tons of video footage of him sitting on a rock eating caramel corn out of a bowl that we had left for him. It would get stuck to his face and he would methodically pick it off with his little raccoon fingers. Now *that* was entertainment!

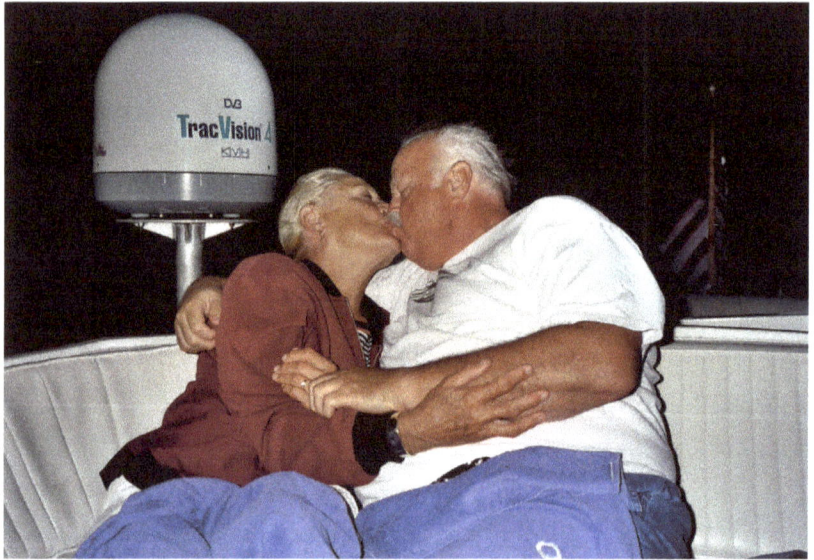

A kiss in the Keys

Bruce's life in the studio, sometimes hectic and around the clock, was made possible because we would take time off to travel, go out on the boat, to the Keys, to Sweden. I think this was an important part of his success. He recharged his batteries. We both did. The sun and the water really did it for us.

We looked after each other

• • •

Roberta, my brother Jim, and I went to India in 1991, and again in 1992. The 1991 journey was Roberta's first trip to India; she had accepted a job teaching music at my old school, Woodstock. She fell in love with it immediately. "The minute we got off the plane, the smell of India hit me and I knew I was hooked," she says. "It was somehow a mixture of petrol, cow dung, incense, spices, and thousands of years of history. I was entranced. The streets, the masses of people, the ancient, ancient culture. America is like a baby Swiss village compared to this. I ended up living in India for sixteen years. I still miss it."

Roberta and I in our North Indian Salwar Kameez

It was always good to be back in India with Jim. He was born there. And of course it was home to both of us. In Delhi, the three of us piled into a white Ambassador car with Raju the driver and took off for the dusty Rajasthani desert, to Jaipur and Udaipur. We stayed at the exquisite Lake Palace. Built in 1743, it was pretty new for India. It faced east so the people living there could pray to the sun god Surya. We went to see where the beautiful Marwari horses were being bred. I really wanted to bring one back to LA.

In Jaipur we stayed at the Rambagh Palace, once a royal hunting lodge. Everything was a startling contrast of extreme rawness and extreme luxury. At one point in the trip, I told Raju to stop at this little not-even-a-village off the road—it was really just a clan of people in the desert. They had one cow and a few goats, and lived in huts made of mud and straw. The women wore colorful, tattered saris. They had beautiful faces and dark eyes. One hid her blind child behind her. The head of the village came up to the road to see us and was curious about my video camera. I took a short video of him and played it back, audio and all. He smiled a big, toothless grin and the others came to see too. They all laughed. Such happy people living life in such a simple way! It was a lesson for everyone.

Our friend in Delhi, Veena Lal, arranged to have an elaborate *howdah* made for Michael's Neverland elephant Gypsy. Made of red silk, it was embellished with gold thread embroidered by hand. We shipped it to LA and both Michael and Gypsy loved it.

Indonesia was next, with our dear friend Kathy Buckley, Rod Temperton's wife, for company. We met up with her in the Singapore Airlines VIP lounge and started our adventure. Roberta and Kathy went river-rafting on a Grade-5 river in Bali (Jim and I stayed safely onshore and filmed them bouncing over the rapids). We saw the *Kecak*, an unforgettable performance of native dance, drama, and rhythmic verse, a kind of ancient, Indonesian beat-boxing. Kathy ate Balinese Nasi Goreng at practically every meal, including breakfast! We finished the trip with a stay at the legendary Raffles Hotel, sipping Singapore Slings.

Bruce stayed home in Moorpark with the animals and his studio. Judy Kelley moved in and looked after everyone. I called him every night.

· · ·

Bruce was thrilled when he once again had the opportunity to work with Sérgio Mendes on his album *Brasileiro*, which would go on to win a Grammy for Best World Music. What fantastic music, and Sérgio is one of the nicest guys ever. We enjoyed many delicious gourmet dinners at the home he shared with his wife Gracinha in Encino. Gracinha is an amazing cook and an incredible singer. We were always served the best of Brazilian cuisine. They were living in this beautiful house, which at one time had been a love nest for Clark Gable and Carol Lombard. We were there one Christmas, and Roberta and I slipped off to the bathroom at one point. I said to her, "Just imagine. Clark Gable sat here!"

The house was constructed of adobe in the Spanish style. The actor Harrison Ford, once a carpenter, built Sérgio a recording studio on the property in 1970. How sad it was that the entire house was destroyed in the 1994 earthquake. Sérgio, Gracinha, and their two sons were very fortunate to have escaped with their lives. But they all carry on and are still performing. We had a great time when they came with their band to perform in Orlando. We sat near the front and Sérgio, on stage with a microphone, and Bruce, in his seat, started a dialogue back and forth. Sérgio would say something in Swedish and Bruce would say something in Portuguese, and then they would both laugh. The audience was puzzled, but laughed right along with them anyway.

• • •

Swedish jazz trombonist Nils Landgren and his musicians (known collectively as the "Funk Unit") came to Moorpark in 1992 to record his album *Red Horn*. (Nils actually plays a red trombone custom-made for him by Yamaha.) The music they did was not just funk but also R&B and jazz: "blue-eyed soul." We had such a great time, all of us being Swedish. We even had crayfish parties—*Kräftskiva*—which involved a lot of eating, drinking, and singing. Nils brought over Swedish engineer Leif Allansson who, with his wife Margareta, have also been dear friends for all these decades, as have Siedah and Erik Nuri, Bernie and Claire Grundman, Chuck Wild, Bernard Lohr (engineer for ABBA and Benny Andersson) and his wife Ulli, Allen and Ann Sides, Ken and Beryl Nordine, the whole Chicago gang and so many more. Friends from our music and boating world—and from Sweden, of course—balanced it all out. We were very lucky.

• • •

Bruce was scheduled to be at Record One Studios in Sherman Oaks on January 17th, 1994, to start Michael's next album *HIStory: Past, Present and Future* but at 4:30 AM a 6.7 earthquake shook the entirety of Los Angeles and beyond. This was the Northridge earthquake. Over 60 people lost their lives but it would have been much worse if it happened during waking hours. The shaking was felt as far away as San Diego and Las Vegas. It caused the greatest damage in the United States since the 1906 San Francisco earthquake and it was one of the world's most expensive natural disasters, costing over $35 billion. There were two large aftershocks immediately following and over 10,000 aftershocks later.

We were very fortunate to suffer no damage to our home. However, we lived in fear because the aftershocks went on for days. For the first few nights, Bruce and I, Teddy, our young Great Dane, and Zack, our Border Collie, slept on the folded-down seats of our Bronco parked in the driveway. Our dogs always knew when an earthquake was coming. They would get nervous, run around looking for something, and start to howl.

The dogs of my childhood in Nagaland did that too. One evening, it was just getting dark out and our dog Keto alerted us, howling. There was an 8.0 point earthquake coming. I remember the servants calmly but quickly running through the bungalow to blow out the kerosene lamps in every room so the house wouldn't ignite. All my siblings were away at boarding school, so it was just me, my mom and dad, and the servants. My parents were very matter of fact about it, calmly getting everyone out of the house. Once outside, I felt like I couldn't stand up any more because the ground was moving so fast. So I fell down and clutched the grass, clinging for dear life. I will never forget that. I have hated earthquakes ever since.

But that home also sustained no damage. We did, however, have a reservoir made out of concrete behind the bungalow. It cracked, causing water to splash out, the same way the water splashed out of our pool in Moorpark during the Northridge quake.

Michael's home in Encino was quite safe, but the family estate in Hayvenhurst had considerable damage and everyone had to move to a rented house. The three-story apartment building across the alley in back of Record One was seriously damaged. As a result, Michael decided to move the *HIStory* project and several days later Bruce was off to the Hit Factory in New York.

• • •

Lisa-Marie Presley and Michael were married in May of 1994. She was often at the studio during the making of the *HIStory* album. They were really happy together and were holding hands all the time. It was precious to see. Bruce said in an interview: *"This marriage is not for commercial purposes. It's a serious thing and I'm glad to see him happy finally. Lisa Marie is great, they feel very good together. They are inseparable. She comes very often to the studio. It feels good to me seeing that, because of that relationship Michael has changed."*

Eddie Germano owned the Hit Factory on West 54th Street in New York. We had known he and his wife, Janice, for years. Wonderful people! We still have the golf cart they gave us with "West Viking Studios" and our viking ship logo painted on the front. Bruce and Eddie were good friends and Bruce loved the Hit Factory. "This is the best studio in the world… for real," he once said. *HIStory* was a double album that included Michael's greatest hits along with new material. A lot of people contributed to that album. And the studio gang was there: Brad Buxer, Michael Boddiker, Rene Moore, Brian Vibberts, Andrew Scheps, Matt Forger, Brad Sundberg, Craig Johnson, and many more. Some of the new songs were very different from Michael's previous work—edgier, angrier. Bruce co-wrote "2Bad" and "This Time Around" with Michael, Dallas Austin, and Rene Moore, and he produced, recorded, and mixed them as well. Both those songs had relentless, driving rhythms.

But the gorgeous ballads with full orchestra were the big thing for him on this album. He used the same studio setup he had used forty years earlier with the Chicago Symphony Orchestra. Michael recorded these deeply personal songs straight through, in one take, live with the orchestra.

Of the experience, Bruce wrote: *"When Michael finished recording "Have You Seen My Childhood" and the Charlie Chaplin song "Smile" with the orchestra, he asked me if he could go out in the studio and meet the musicians. Over the studio talkback I asked Jeremy Lubbock (arranger and conductor) if Michael could come out to meet the orchestra. 'Of course,' he said. 'Absolutely!' During the recording, the entire orchestra had been listening to Michael sing through their individual headphones. When Michael walked out in the studio to meet the musicians, they gave him a standing ovation. Every member of the 50-piece orchestra stood up and tapped their music stands with their bows as loud as they could. Jeremy stood on the conductor's podium and also applauded as loud as he could. I was applauding too, in the control room, as loud as I could. Michael was thrilled."*

Bruce and Michael

The orchestra for "Childhood" and "Smile" at the Hit Factory

• • •

Roberta flew in from New Delhi to do sound design on the album, turning ancient Indian percussion into funk grooves. Of the experience, she wrote:

"The first time I met Michael, he was standing in a studio doorway at the Hit Factory in New York. I was at the piano, playing the crazy fast Gigue from Bach's B-Flat Major Partita. Keyboard player Brad Buxer was my only audience, or so I thought. Finally, looking up I saw Michael and realized he had been standing there, listening. He so enjoyed the surprise on my face; we both burst out laughing. He also enjoyed the Bach. I'll never forget the radiance in his eyes, like they were dancing . . .

I had come from New Delhi to New York to bring 'funky tabla' grooves to the HIStory *project. My dad had been inspired by listening to Indian music while waiting for his vindaloo in a little Indian restaurant on a strip mall in LA. There were moments of pure Motown in that music and he had a brainstorm to create loops using the Indian percussion and that soulful energy. Michael loved the idea. So, armed with instruments, dance bells, finger cymbals, CDs, and tapes, I traveled to the other side of the globe to make some music for Michael.*

A few hours after the Bach encounter, my dad said, 'Come on, let's go meet him!' I gathered up my Indian gear and we went into Michael's room; a space at the Hit Factory that he used for songwriting and meetings. It was just the three of us. Michael was warm and welcoming, soft-spoken and very sincere. Even though the setting was relaxed, he seemed to exude a kind of quiet kinetic energy. It was striking and unforgettable, and it filled the room.

Like Santa Claus from a faraway land, I pulled my treasures out of their brown paper bags and handed them to Michael, one by one. Everything aroused his curiosity and interest, but it was the dance bells that fascinated him. These were a gift to Michael from my dear friend, Harash. They had been worn by dancers in his family and were of the Kathak *style of North India, a dance form that tells stories from the great epic poems of Hinduism. The design hasn't changed for hundreds of years: leather straps that buckle around the ankle and calf, hundreds of small, round bells sewn on by hand. These were old and had signs of wear and tear. A few of the bells were spotted with rust from living through many monsoons. They had character and rhythmic spirit. Michael held the bells in his hands and was quiet. Slowly turning them over and over, he suddenly shook them and smiled. 'Thank you,' he said softly. Shaking them again, his eyes lit up and he said, 'We have to sample these!'*

We talked about India. He had long had an interest, having heard my mother's stories of her incredible childhood in Nagaland during the British Raj, and he was curious to know about my experiences in modern India. But he was concerned about the problems of the country: poverty, population, education, and health care.

Michael asked me to choose some classical piano CDs for him to listen to. I suggested the French Impressionists, in particular the Debussy Preludes, exquisite soundscapes with titles like 'What the West Wind Saw,' 'Sunken Cathedral' and 'Sounds and Scents Mingle in the Evening Air.' He loved the imagery and wanted to hear the music.

Throughout the meeting it was easy to see that Michael was an intelligent, sensitive and serious individual. There was an aura of integrity about him. The word noble comes to mind.

I was teamed up with Scott 'You Got It!' Pittinsky, a brilliant and energetic young sound design whiz-kid. We turned his funky little studio off of Times Square, 'Compound Sound,' into a 'Funky Tabla Loop Factory.' The room resounded with recordings of Indian drums, vocals, sitar, santoor, shennai, bamboo flute, old 'filmi' music, Bollywood, Bhangra and the folk music of Rajasthan, the Punjab and South India . . . just to get the vibe going. My funk inspiration came from only two sources: James Brown and the Brothers Johnson.

Once the stage was set in our ears, we got down to the business of actual loop making and worked fourteen hours a day, seven days a week. We sampled those magnificent dance bells, the finger cymbals, and all the instruments I had brought from Delhi in Studio One at the Hit Factory. Then we'd go back to Scott's studio and do the crafting. We ordered food, sometimes using discount coupons. We were not like those certain members of the project who ordered Kobe beef every night and put it on Michael's tab.

Scott put the dance bells onto a keyboard so that I, with Rachmaninoff fingers, could play them. Soulful funk met the history and mystery of India. I gave each loop a name: 'Bombay Twilight,' 'Calcutta Backstreet,' 'Gandhi's Dream,' 'Bengal Tiger,' and so on. The first DAT was delivered to Michael; he loved it and wanted more. We made more than twenty in all.

I went in the studio for two weeks and came out two months later. Needless to say, this was the experience of a lifetime. The highest standards conceivable permeated every facet of this project. People work like this for Michael because he is an artist who truly inspires. Before I left he autographed a photo for me. He wrote, 'Thank you for your loyal efforts. Love, Michael.' Loyalty is no small thing to him.

Looking back on this time with Michael, I am struck primarily by three things: his very eclectic interest in music, his unaffected personality, and the extraordinary contrast between Michael the person and Michael the performer. I have seen this before in great artists; a quiet and almost unassuming self that becomes utterly transformed while performing, whether it's in rehearsal, in the studio, or on a stage. They seem to 'channel' the very essence of the musical power, energy, and meaning. It doesn't take a gregarious or aggressive personality to make an outstanding performer, but it does require a musically honest, courageous and open soul. Michael had this tenfold; he was like a kind of high-voltage conduit, charged with electric, musical truth."

CHAPTER FIVE

CONNECTICUT

During the *HIStory* project, Bruce lived in a luxurious suite at the Westbury Hotel on Madison Avenue. I would fly to New York every couple of weeks to see him, but once Michael decided he didn't want to go back to the West Coast, we knew it was time to make the move permanent. We found a lovely farm on twenty-eight acres in Roxbury, Connecticut, just a train ride from Manhattan.

Our new home in Roxbury, a town that was settled in 1713

Since Bruce was busy working in the studio with Michael, it was up to me to get us moved east. I sold our ranch in California, complete with its own recording studio and animal housings, and made arrangements with Bekins Van Lines to pack us up and get us moved. I had to find homes for our many chickens, geese, ducks, and other animals. Then I had to figure out how to get twenty-three cats and four horses moved to the East Coast.

I flew to Connecticut to get the house ready for the movers. Then I went back to California to make arrangements for shipping the horses east. I purchased a used motor home in hopes of transporting our twenty-three cats, but it broke down before we even got it to our ranch. Never one to give up, I chartered a plane to fly the cats east. Javier and Maricela Cardona, who worked for us for years, volunteered to fly along with them. So Judy Kelley, who also worked for us, helped corral all the cats and put them into cat crates and onto the plane. When they stopped to refuel, people heard that it was a plane full of cats and wanted to see them. Javier told them to keep their distance, saying, "These are very famous cats!" This cat flight earned me a mention in *W* magazine.

The final step was to get Teddy, our Great Dane, and Zack the Border Collie to our new home. It was up to Judy and I to drive them across the country. We had a very pleasant journey and were especially happy that all the motels we stayed at allowed dogs. The real godsend was that Javier and Maricela, their kids, and Judy all moved to Connecticut with us. It was such a relief to have them there. They were like family.

We made it ours right away

We built the cathouse to match the New England barn, complete with cupola

My huge new warmblood, Tiny's Ticket

The property was truly picturesque in that New England way: vast fields lined with trees. There was even a pond with fish and frogs. We had a huge eight-stall horse barn with an office, feed room, bathroom, shower stall for the horses, and a foaling stall. On the second floor was a guest apartment and a hay loft. We built an aviary for our new collection of chickens and geese. I even had some Guinea fowl. One of them poked me in the eye, so after that, when going into their pen I had to wear goggles.

We hired an architect to design a cat house to match the style of the barn, cupola and all. These were happy cats having all that acreage of woods and fields to explore, weather permitting. They all came in every night to relax, eat and sleep in the luxury and safety of their New England cat house.

Our home was huge and elegant. Bruce put a studio on the lower ground floor; I took one of the main floor rooms and turned it into an India room. It had a gun cabinet, an elephant table with Bruce's collection of small carved elephants, brass trays and figurines, an old side saddle, a gramophone, silk wall hangings, and a statue of the Hindu god Ganesha, remover of obstacles.

We have a statue of St Francis of Assisi that has always relocated with us, as well as a "Viking runestone" made for us by my crazy brother Jim. He engraved a message in his own version of Viking hieroglyphics that translated as "Here two days journey from the sea, Swedien the brave, kin to Fritjof and master of Odin, with his woman, did take land from the savages with halberd, fire and death. Ave Maria. West Viking 1980" painstakingly chiseled onto a many-hundred pound slab of stone. He hauled it from Escondido to Moorpark. And it has traveled with us to every home since... by very annoyed movers.

The local social life and culture in and around Roxbury was what you would expect from sophisticated rural Connecticut: it included Henry Kissinger, Stephen Sondheim, Dustin Hoffman, Richard Widmark, Walter Matthau and the like. Needless to say, we attended and hosted many dinner parties. Sandy Lean lived not far away. She was the famous director David Lean's widow. And guess what? She went to Woodstock!

• • •

Michael had met Javier and Marciela Cardona, who worked for us at our home in Moorpark the year before. The Cardonas had three terrific kids: Gabriel, Xavier, and Cytlally. It was around Christmastime that Michael had as his guest one of his nephews who had recently lost his mother. Since Michael was occupied in the studio, he figured this young boy needed the companionship of kids of his own age. So Michael asked his secretary Evvy to call me and ask if the three young Cardona children could come from their house in Connecticut for a few days' visit with his nephew in New York. They all came and Michael put the entire family up in a first-class hotel.

While they were in New York, Michael treated all the kids to a shopping spree at FAO Schwartz. Of course, the entire outing was safely escorted by his security people. As a crowning holiday touch, Michael arranged for a Christmas party with an enormous Christmas tree, complete with Santa Claus, in huge Studio One at the Hit Factory. Wonderful food and a fun time was had by all.

• • •

In 1996 we went to Japan with Bernie and Claire Grundman. Bruce and Bernie did master classes in Tokyo and Claire and I bummed around. Bernie was a Swede from Minneapolis, which made it old-home week. He ended up opening a studio in Tokyo that is still thriving today.

1997 proved to be an even busier year.

In February we went to New York for the Grammys at Madison Square Garden. Once again a thrill, and so wonderful to have the Grammys in The Big Apple. And now it was just an hour and a half from home. Bruce was nominated and won a Grammy for his work on Quincy's new album *Jook Joint*, which got to #1 on the Billboard jazz albums chart. Bruce shared the award with fellow engineers Al Schmitt, Tommy Vicari, and Francis Buckley. Quincy gathered all his music friends and put that album together to celebrate his 50th year in music. It's a star-studded reunion of the absolute best players and singers. Sarah Vaughan was on it, and so was Miles Davis, Ray Charles, Charlie Parker, Dizzie Gillespie, Billy Eckstine, Nancy Wilson, and Toots Thielemans as well as Stevie Wonder, Chaka Khan, Bono, Brandy, Phil Collins, Babyface, Barry White, and our gang: Siedah, JR, Greg Phillinganes, Patti, Rod, and many more. Bruce loved working on that album. It was truly old home week!

Next we were off to Mexico City, where Bruce had been invited by Chris Adams of *Studio Sound International* magazine to speak at the Latin-American Pro Audio and Music Expo. We had a great time; they made us both feel so at home. Bruce had a lot of fans there. He did a CD signing at Tower Records, a four-story building, and the line of people that wanted to meet him went all the way down four stories and around the block. He was interviewed on a morning TV show, *Un*

Nuevo Dia, and his favorite part was the Mariachi band. One night we went to dinner at the home of Lupita and Ricardo Murguia and the chicken mole tamales were so delicious that after we got back to the States Bruce contacted our friend Sérgio García and asked him to send some moles to our house. That wasn't possible from Mexico but he had a friend in Chicago cook the moles and ship them to us in Connecticut. Bruce often got what he wanted. Delicious!

• • •

Last, but not in any way least, was a trip in November back to Nagaland. There was a celebration of 125 years of missionary work in the Naga Hills. We were so excited to be going back! My sister Audrey, her husband Roger, and I flew to meet Roberta in Delhi. Jim was sure we wouldn't get in, so he stayed behind. It was a much regretted decision.

Nagaland had been a restricted area for many years. Roberta had made some Naga friends in Delhi, Rev. Ricky and Viring Medom. Ricky's full first name is Noulezhalie. He is from the Angami tribe and his brother-in-law Khekiye Sema, who was an administrative officer of the government of Nagaland, is from the Sema tribe, now called Sümi. My father worked with many tribes but we lived with the Aos and the Semas. From 1873 -2011 all non-indigenous people were required to obtain a permit to enter Nagaland, so we met up with the Nagas at Roberta's apartment in Delhi and got our permits and paperwork together. We were so very happy to meet these people; it was like meeting long-lost family. They, of course, knew all about my dad and our family and his years of work with the Nagas.

Once we landed in Dimapur, there were Indian Gypsys (SUVs) and drivers waiting to take us to Kohima, the capital city of Nagaland, where the festival was to take place. We were Rev. Anderson's people and were quickly aware of the significance of that honor. He was still a legend and well-remembered by the Naga people. He loved them deeply for his entire life.

The festival was so impressive! All the various tribes had a presentation, and much of it was music. The Nagas are natural musicians. They can be sitting in a group and just break into perfect four-part harmony. At one point, all four of us were brought up onstage and wrapped in ceremonial shawls as an acknowledgement of my parent's contributions. Some of my dad's tools and books he had translated into tribal languages were in a museum, along with my mother's old sewing machine. There have been many enduring honors made to my parents, especially by the Sümis in Aizuto. They built the Anderson Theological College in 1993, and in 2021 the Women's Ministry built the Edna Anderson Garden in memory of my mother.

Audrey and I with a young Naga—we were home

After the festival, members of the Ao church drove us to Mokokchung and Impur, where we had once lived. Audrey had spent more years there than I had. But it was indescribable to be back in those remote hills, looking at those beautiful smiling faces, once again hearing the music of their language—the language that I first spoke. We walked and talked and sat around fires in the winter chill, kept warm by our shawls, woven by the women in the villages. And suddenly there in front of me was my sweet Tsungkumla, my *ayah* from over fifty years ago. She was very old now, 89, but had come on foot from her village, climbing over two hills to see us. She called me Beeseelah! It was a joyous and tearful reunion.

The Sema Nagas event for the Anderson family

The Semas came and took us to Aizuto, my childhood home, where they had prepared an elaborate event for us. There was an outdoor performance of traditional singing and dancing, with songs that had the Anderson name woven into the words. Our old bungalow had been renovated with modern plumbing, and everything was thought of for our Western comfort, including the food. The Naga diet consists of a lot of fermented food, which none of us had ever taken to. But we were fed the most delicious grilled fish and vegetables. Khekiye's sister Ghotoli did a wonderful job of taking care of us. We felt so loved by all the Nagas.

"It was an unforgettable experience," says Roberta. "In the town of Impur, home to the tribe of the Aos, my mom stood alone on a platform in front of thousands of Nagas, and in their native tongue, with great flourish and gesture, she shouted 'Welcome, Ao Nagas, to the celebration!' She was home."

•   •   •

The next year, Bruce and I decided to take a little well-deserved time off with another trip to Sweden. While there, we stayed at a small seaside *stuga* (a cottage) on the Baltic. It was heaven! Calm and quiet with the sea air wafting in the windows and Swedish birds in the trees. My cousin Birgitta had loaned us her cell phone as there was no phone at the cottage. One night at around 2 AM the phone rang and it was Herbie Hancock calling from New York, saying, "Bruce, you have to come back to New York and mix my new album *Gershwin's World*!" So back to New York and Sony Studios we went.

Bruce and Herbie had known each other for years, working together with Quincy on the *Sounds and Stuff Like That* and *Back on the Block* albums. *Gershwin's World* was a compilation of music written by George and Ira Gershwin and their contemporaries. Herbie gathered a gallery of artists to perform on it, including Joni Mitchell, Kathleen Battle, Stevie Wonder, Wayne Shorter, Chick Corea, and the Orpheus Chamber Orchestra. He would win two Grammys for that album.

Roberta later ran into Herbie backstage at the National Center for Performing Arts in Bombay, India. Herbie had just finished a concert there and Roberta was going to be performing Schubert's song cycle *Die Schöne Mullerin* with American tenor Kevin Hanrahan the next night. She told Herbie that she thought his improvisation of the Ravel *Adagio from the Piano Concerto in G* on the Gershwin album was as good as the original. His eyes popped. "Really?" he said.

• • •

In 2000 Bruce was working with the talented producer and composer Andres Levine at our small studio in Connecticut. One project they were commissioned to do for Sony of France was to record the French singer Cyrius Martinez in Cuba. So off we went to Havana.

We stayed at the legendary Hotel Nacional, which at one time had been owned by Al Capone and had a history of guests from Marlene Dietrich to Lucky Luciano. Our room was haunted by a lady who sang a bolero in Spanish right by our bed. When we inquired about this, we were told she had often been seen walking the halls. I wasn't frightened, having had some ghost experiences of my own back in India. There was a *dak bunaglow* (government rest house) in an Assamese village called Bymo that was haunted. The District Commissioner told my father, "Don't ever take your family there overnight!" But my father stayed once and in the middle of the night a horrible smell permeated the room and an iridescent green horse's head appeared. He was terrified. Others had seen it too. It was called "The Bymo Ghost." The singing Cuban lady was pretty tame in comparison.

At the Hotel Nacional in Havana, Cuba
with producer Andres Levin and Ileana Padron

The studio we would be working in was named EGREM. It was very old, built in the 1940s—and it sounded extraordinary. Nat King Cole and Josephine Baker had recorded there. Bruce always said it was like stepping back in time. The Cuban musicians and singers, including Cyrius, the singer/songwriter, were fantastic. There was an old, somewhat battered Steinway grand there but it had been lovingly cared for, was in perfect tune and had a warm, rich sound... and the piano player was amazing. That sums up a lot of our Cuban musical experience: The equipment is old but cared for, and the musicians are exceptional. Thanks to Andres Levin and his wife Ileana, we came to know and love Cuba. Mickey and Randy also came down at one point to join us.

As a birthday present for Bruce, I had arranged to charter a sixty-foot Italian yacht that was berthed at the Hemingway Marina in Havana. We and our guests were all going on a snorkeling trip. The day before we were to set sail, the travel agent asked to see all of our passports. She then informed me that one of our group would not be allowed to go on the trip because of "passport complications." I was furious so I canceled the trip.

But I love Cuba and the Cuban people. When we had a free evening we would go to one of the many small clubs to hear some excellent music. On several occasions the MC or band leader would introduce Bruce from the stage. One of the arrangers who was working on the project was a large man with a terrific sense of humor. With a smile, he would pat his tummy and then pat Bruce's tummy and say "cementerio de pollo," which is Spanish for chicken cemetery.

· · ·

In 2001 we all went to the Hit Factory in Miami for some sessions with Michael for his new album *Invincible*. We had gorgeous hotel suites on the Bal Harbour beach. I'll never forget the big stretch limo that pulled up in front of the studio the first day. People thought it was Michael, so everyone was excited. Instead, a guy with long gray hair and jeans got out. It was the label guy from Sony! Michael, of course, arrived in an ordinary van. His kids, Paris and Prince, were there as well, and we all sat in the control room together. They were so sweet! Michael was always keeping a watchful eye out for them.

Still looking for ways to mingle in society without being recognized, Michael found new inspiration from Roberta's Indian wardrobe. "I had just come in from Delhi where I was living at the time," she explains, "and was wearing my Indian clothes: salwar kameez, a Bengali embroidered chunni/scarf, and chappals with 24 karat gold earrings and bangles. The next morning Michael called my room and told me he loved me and he really loved my clothes! Then he asked if I would find someone to make him some Indian clothes and told me to call Evvy, his assistant, to get his measurements. When I went back to Delhi, I found some young designers, Abdul and Payal—he was Muslim and she was Hindu—who were perfect for the task. They went all out for Michael: kurtas, churidar, turbans, slippers, the whole thing. Patterns were made out of newspapers. The "Zari" work (bead stitching) was done by men sitting on the floor, with the fabric on a huge low table covered with hundreds of gold and silver beads waiting to be sewn on, each by hand, to create elaborate designs. They even stitched his signature armband onto the sleeve of one of the kurtas. A cobbler with hand-made traditional silk slippers for Michael came on a train from the Rajasthani desert. We had Indian outfits made for young Paris and Prince. We also sent books and Indian music CDs, incense, and even a little toy rickshaw for the kids. Michael loved everything and wore the clothes as disguises when he wanted to go outside and not be mobbed."

Kurta, turban and chappals hand-made for Michael in New Delhi

• • •

On September 7th and 10th 2001, Michael's 30th Anniversary Celebration concert was held at Madison Square Garden to honor his thirty years as a solo entertainer. It was a star-studded event and it sold out in two hours—nearly 20,000 seats. There were some tickets that went for $10,000; that included both the show and dinner with Michael. We were there for the performance on the 7th and sat in the second row on the side, not far from Michael and Elizabeth Taylor, Macaulay Culkin, and Katherine Jackson, Michael's mother. Once again, it was almost surreal to be sitting there at Michael's live performance with thousands of screaming fans. Our life with him was in the quiet of the studio, where things were crafted, meticulously, by a fairly small group of people. That was where the hit songs were created. And here we were in the bright lights and euphoria of the people who loved him, who knew every word of every song, dancing with him, connecting to his incredible energy. We were so proud of him and so grateful to be part of his team.

Bruce stayed in New York the next day, but I went back to Connecticut because we had guests coming in from Sweden. Bjorn Asplind, who was helping Bruce with his first book *Make Mine Music*, was coming to visit with his daughter Linn. They were planning to take the train into New York and go sightseeing on Tuesday the 11th.

I had the TV on that morning when the horrible news started coming in. It was absolutely unfathomable. I called Roberta in New Delhi where it was already Tuesday night. She was watching the news there too, in shock and disbelief, as was the whole world.

What we didn't know was that Michael was supposed to be at a meeting at the World Trade Center that very morning. But he missed the meeting because he overslept after a late night talk with his mother and siblings. She called him the next morning to see if he was okay and he told her he was because of her keeping him up late the night before! Imagine. The whole thing was such a tragedy.

Bjorn remembers 9/11 this way: *"Linn and I arrived at Kennedy airport from Sweden on September 9th to go to Connecticut and stay at Bruce and Bea's. We stayed in the guest apartment above the barn. Bruce and I were planning to work on the book until Saturday the 15th when Linn and I would go home. On Monday we worked on the book. Bruce was busy on Tuesday so our plan was to take the train into Manhattan and go shopping.*

I got up just before nine o'clock, showered, and turned on the TV, but kept the volume off and had some breakfast. On the TV, I saw a skyscraper burning about 10-15 floors from the top. My first thought was, well now they've made a new movie and the skyscraper is on fire. How realistic it looks. Yes, yes, everything can be done with the new technology. The image remained and then I saw that it was ABC News so I turned up the volume. 'A small plane has flown in and collided with the building. Emergency personnel are on their way,' said a voice. Should we really go in? I thought, and decided to call Bruce in the main house.

'Hello, Bruce, there has been an accident with a plane. Maybe we should not go in?'

'Manhattan is big, you don't need to visit the accident site. I'll turn on the TV,' Bruce replied. It was now a few minutes after 9. We were still on the phone, each standing in front of a TV as plane number two comes and drives straight into the second tower. We were both so shocked that nothing was said for a long time. 'I don't think we're going,' I finally say. 'I agree; wait a minute, I'll come over to you,' said Bruce.

After about 45 minutes, Bruce came and told me that Michael Jackson had called. He was completely horrified. He was in a hotel in New York and all the flights were down so he couldn't leave. Michael's team had tried to book a helicopter but there was a total no-fly zone across the US. What is going on? Will there be a war? A thousand thoughts ran through my head.

I tried to call home to Sweden but it didn't work. After a while, a good friend from Sweden called so I could tell him that we hadn't gone into Manhattan. I called the airline and wondered, how long will there be a flight ban? Will I get home on Saturday? They couldn't answer anything. How will I get home?

Bruce, who was used to problem-solving in the studio, said calmly 'Björn, if the flight doesn't work from here, I'll drive you to Canada.' We didn't have to go to Canada. We flew back to Sweden on Saturday the 15th. On board the plane, waiting for takeoff, it was completely silent and the atmosphere was very tense. Then people started crying and screaming. The flight attendants ran in the aisles and asked if there were any doctors or psychologists on board. Unfortunately, many had been seized by panic attacks."

• • •

Two months later, we also were on a plane to Sweden. In November of that year, Bruce was to receive an Honorary Doctorate from the Luleå University of Technology, presented under the ruling of King Carl XVI Gustaf. We got on an international flight to Stockholm. Needless to say, the security was military-level. Bruce and I, my Swedish cousin Birgitta, our Norwegian studio friend Trond Braaten, and Roberta, who had flown in from Delhi, met in Birgitta's town of Ockelbo and drove way up north into the town of Luleå, which is located just seventy miles south of the Arctic Circle. Only the Swedes would schedule this very formal ceremony in such a location in the winter.

Bruce received an Honorary Doctorate in Sweden in 2001

What a great honor for Bruce! This really meant a lot to him. The solemn and stately white-tie ceremony was held in the Luleå Cathedral, whose original building harkened back to 1667. We were put up at the circa 1898 Amber Hotel, not too far from the cathedral, so we decided to walk to the event. Not an easy task as we were dressed in formal attire and making our way in dress shoes and heels on icy streets in the dark!

Men in long velvet robes and regalia presented the ribbon-bound diploma, ring, and hat to each awardee as tokens of honor. The Swedish tradition of wearing a doctoral hat arose in the late 16th century. It's a handmade black, pleated top hat with a gold buckle on the front. It is held over the head of the recipient for ten long, silent seconds, then slowly placed on the head to applause from the audience. Bruce was so proud of this moment in his life. His Swedish ancestors would have been proud too.

Following the ceremony there was an elaborate banquet with all sorts of Swedish dignitaries and also many of our Swedish relatives. There was a lot of music; everything from polkas for dancing to Roberta performing the piano music of Swedish classical composers. One of the other awardees that year was Yngve Bergqvist, owner and founder of the Icehotel, a hotel of ice and snow built from the ground up every year in Jukkasjärvi, 200 kilometers north of the Arctic Circle. People come from all over the world to dine, drink, and sleep in this astounding building made of ice. (It melts every summer and is rebuilt when the freeze hits.) When Yngve heard Roberta performing Swedish music, he suggested she play a concert in the Icehotel. But then they realized that a piano might not fare very well in sub-zero temperatures.

Bruce's Grammys

Each album meant a lot to Bruce

CHAPTER SIX

FLORIDA

As much as we loved the Connecticut countryside and the buzz of New York City nearby, we decided it was time for warmer climes. Friends led us to Ocala, Florida and a 26-acre horse farm. Ocala was big blue sky country, open spaces, lots of horses… and no snow! The move was easier this time, just down the coast and into mild and sunny north-central Florida. I found a huge, open house with a pool for Bruce as he loved to swim. And he found himself a fire-engine red Ford 1982 diesel pickup truck with a sun visor. It was his pride and joy.

Now we had a huge Florida-style concrete block barn to keep the horses cool in the heat and sun. We built a chicken coop and a cat house, of course, and the good times began.

Our Border Collie, Gordie, came with us to Florida. Our beautiful Fawn Great Dane, Teddy who we had since Moorpark passed away in Connecticut. He was eleven years old, very old for a Dane. That was a very sad day for me. Our Danes lived long lives compared to the average, but it is never long enough.

We started looking for our next Dane and found him in a very unlikely place. The owners of the DeConna Ice Cream Company in Ocala were also breeding Great Danes. They had a young guy, a Mantle, up for adoption. The Mantle Dane is black and white and is huge—they can grow up to weigh 180 pounds. We named him Boo. What a beautiful, sweet dog. He wouldn't be hanging around Hollywood studios or have a microphone in his face or try to stay standing during an earthquake. Instead, he was a fun in the sun Florida Dane. We made many wonderful friends in Ocala.

Sunny Florida with Boo and Gordy

When word got out that we had moved to Florida, some people were thinking that Bruce had retired. That word was never in his vocabulary!

• • •

"Every time I looked at a record I liked, it would be engineered and mixed by Bruce Swedien. I was like, 'Who is this guy? I want this guy.' So I tracked him down and he was like, 'I want to do something with her. I know exactly what she needs. I'm coming in.' And it made a huge difference."—Jennifer Lopez

Jennifer loved Bruce

As Bruce told it, "*Bea and I were enormously relieved when one day, after we had moved into our new place in Florida, the phone rang. I picked it up and it was my old pal Benny Medina. It was great to hear from him. At the time Benny was Jennifer Lopez's manager.*

Benny asked me if I would be available to work on Jennifer's new album for Sony Music. Needless to say, I asked, 'When do we start?'

I had heard a lot about Jennifer Lopez, but what attracted me to her album project was, first of all, I loved the sound of her voice, but equally important is that I had heard that she was not afraid to work hard on a project. I love to work hard on all my projects and with that kind of commitment from an artist, I felt that I could help take Jennifer to a new level of musical and sonic excellence.

Jennifer Lopez has another aspect to her skills as an artist that I think is very rare, and it really appeals to me. I have recorded many of the very best artists in the industry, but rarely have I seen a performer with the innate naturalness that Jennifer exhibits. She has that same ease and believability, whether she is an actress on the big screen, or a vocalist in the recording studio."

Many of the top recording artists of today possess a spectacular vocal instrument, and have a great deal of style at their command, but often I find myself having a difficult time believing them, either musically or lyrically. Their dexterity and style is very apparent, but is anyone sincere actually there? To me, to be important, a popular song must make a spiritual connection with the listener. Its true value lies not in the vocal acrobatics of the performer, but in what the performer's musical statement declares to the soul of the listener. It's positively wonderful to record a vocal with Jennifer Lopez and then listen to it later and find yourself believing every phrase, every word, every time you listen.

We started work on Jennifer's new album, at The Record Plant in Hollywood. In retrospect, I have a feeling that those sessions were set up to see how we all got along. Of course, we had a great time together, and the song we recorded during those sessions, "You Belong To Me," is, I think, one of the best on the album. Early in the project I learned that Verdine White was on a plane to New York from Los Angeles to play bass on the album. Verdine and his incredible brother Maurice White are old pals from my studio days in Chicago. They are very well known for the legendary band they founded: Earth, Wind & Fire. I first met Maurice at Universal Studios in Chicago when he was a session drummer."

Jennifer and Bruce did three albums together: *This is Me... Then*, *Rebirth*, and her Spanish language album *Como Ama una Mujer*. I was at some of those sessions. It was so inspiring to watch Jennifer work. She has the discipline of a dancer. She was up early, working with her vocal coach, and she was at the studio before anyone else. I remember there was this very good-looking, quiet guy in the control room. I couldn't tell who he was because his face was half-hidden by a cap. Turns out it was Ben Affleck! He was with her every day.

"That one [This Is Me... Then] *was me getting a little more musical and writing a lot more,"* she said. *"I was going through some difficult times, so it just means more to me. Also, the sound of that album, I*

worked with engineer Bruce Swedien. Legendary. The way he recorded my vocals and the way we did things, it was just a whole other process. We took it to the next level and I'm just so proud of that album.

"Listening to it from top to bottom, sonically and the content, it was all exactly what I wanted it to be. It was really me."

• • •

It was book time for both Bruce and me. He was finishing his first book, *Make Mine Music*, and I was starting my first one, *Under the Red Blanket*, about my childhood in India. I had been sharing stories of my unusual upbringing with friends for many years. Everyone said I should write them down, so when my brother Jim and sisters June and Audrey came to Ocala to stay with us, Bruce set up a microphone in the living room and for days we just talked and talked, remembering our days in the Naga Hills. What fun we had as kids and what great memories we shared there in our Ocala living room! Stories of travels, boarding school, and the general mischief missionary kids could get up to in the jungle were all recorded on tape. I wrote about the politics of the time, the impact of World War II, the earthquake in Assam, and the glorious day when Nagaland achieved statehood in India. It was a project that was very close to my heart. I wish my parents could have read it.

Make Mine Music was published in 2003 to critical acclaim. It was so important to Bruce to write this book, which summed up his philosophies and techniques of music-making and recording.

• • •

In 2005 Bruce was invited to Copenhagen as an Ambassador to represent the music industry for the celebration of Hans Christian Andersen's 200th birthday.

We were flown to Copenhagen in first class, put up in a lovely hotel along with "Ambassadors" from many other countries. There was an elegant reception where we all got acquainted.

The following day we were all taken, along with the Queen, on her private train to Odense, Hans Christian Andersen's birthplace. Many of the lovely Danish people lined the railroad tracks waving little Danish flags. Upon arrival we were served an elegant luncheon, after which we toured the museum.

The next night there was a concert in the soccer stadium. We were seated alongside all the Scandinavian Royals, including the Swedish King and Queen.

Tina Turner's incredible performance at this concert brought the house down. Olivia Newton John also entertained, and there was a fantastic group of Chinese children singing. The hosts of the concert were Roger Moore and Harry Belafonte, with close to 30,000 people in attendance. On every seat there was a red satin cushion tied with a green ribbon. When you undid the ribbon, inside was the story of the "Princess and the Pea," along with a small ceramic green bead to represent the pea. Best of all, everyone was allowed to keep the cushions as a souvenir.

The following evening there was a very formal reception in the beautiful old city palace where each one of us was formally presented to the Queen. What an amazing experience! At the same event Bruce and I met three Nobel Prize winners.

The next day we had to fly to Sweden, where Bruce spoke at a seminar in the town of Piteå. Though we had to take three international flights in eight days, we had a wonderful time in spite of the hectic schedule.

While we were still in Copenhagen, we had the good fortune to reconnect with a young Danish engineer, Niels Erik Lund, who had worked with Bruce and Quincy Jones in Los Angeles as an assistant on several album projects. Among them was Quincy's *Sounds and Stuff Like That*, as well as *Blam!* from the Brothers Johnson. Nils and his lovely wife Annette invited Bruce, my Swedish cousin Birgitta Persson, and I to their beautiful seaside home for a delicious dinner. Annette had just given birth to a sweet baby girl two days before. We Scandinavians are a tough lot!

Our customary Swedish vimple (flag) flying in the breeze

When we got back home, we decided that we wanted a smaller property and found a beautiful home on eight acres in Cross Tie Ranches, not far from our other place in Ocala. It had a little forest of trees that created a cool haven of shade in the hot Florida sun.

• • •

Bruce in his Ocala studio at his much loved Harrison console

We also had a barn with two stalls, a tack room, feed room, chicken house and, of course, the obligatory cat house. Not to mention Bruce's studio. Ben Richard built the studio interior and the barn single-handedly. He also created paths from the house and the studio to the barn and through the woods. One of our favorite things to do was to put the dogs into the golf cart and tool around the property and through the woods. Bruce loved coming out to nature after long hours spent closed in with equipment and screens and electricity. The trees and sky were another kind of analog to him.

Ryan Williams, Bruce's assistant, describes the studio this way: *"Bruce transformed an old tractor shed into a state-of-the-art home studio. Designed with impeccable attention to detail by renowned acoustical engineer Art Noxon, it merged rustic charm with cutting-edge acoustics. At the heart of the studio was Bruce's Harrison 32 recording console, a tool that was integral to many of his most iconic albums. This console, together with his carefully curated microphone collection and outboard processing equipment, allowed Bruce to craft his signature sound in a place uniquely his own."*

Bruce loved having his own studio and he always thought it was important that he give back to the recording industry by sharing his experience and wisdom with young engineers and producers. Over the years he had conducted teaching seminars and sessions all over the world: LA, New York, Paris, Helsinki, Stockholm, Gothenburg, Havana, Mexico City, Oslo, Hamburg, Cologne, Munich, Dubai. I was with him for every trip and it was so inspiring to see the next generations of music-makers hang on his every word.

He started his "In the Studio with Bruce Swedien" master classes when we moved to Florida. Bruce had been sitting behind a mixing board for more than forty years. Now it was time to pass on his knowledge. He became an elder statesman of music, traveling the world to receive awards and hold seminars that taught the next generation lessons from his legendary career.

For the classes in Florida, engineers, producers and studio owners would come from all over the world to spend a week with Bruce, learning hands-on recording, mixing, and music appreciation. There were guest speakers too: Engineer Ed Cherney, mastering engineer Bernie Grundman, Martin Kantola of Nordic Audio Labs (who built a microphone for Bruce that had our Viking ship on it), Art Noxon of Acoustic Sciences, audio specialist John Klett, John Jennings of Royer Microphones, to name a few. Bruce took his classes on field trips, too, having them sit in main floor seats to hear the Jacksonville Symphony. He so believed in the acoustical appreciation of the music source.

I did the paperwork for the classes, which was no small task, as well as arranging transportation from Orlando and booking hotels, dates, guest speakers. Ramsees Mechan helped. But it was all a labor of love. The people we met doing the classes were such wonderful people, and many of the friendships have lasted to this day. After the class was over, we would all go out for dinner—Chinese or ribs or seafood. One night we got to our favorite, Sam's Seafood restaurant, just as they were closing. When they saw this bunch of hungry music makers they opened the place for us and fired up the kitchen.

Bruce also was a guest lecturer at Full Sail University, a college located just outside of Orlando that offers degrees in media and entertainment industries. Bruce and I would spend the days in classes, meeting with students and staff, and evenings would be filled with dinners with Full Sail administration and faculty. Garry Jones really made it all happen. Bruce ended up hiring Several Full Sail graduates to work as assistants in our home studio, including Ryan Williams, Nick Valentin, Ramsees Mechan and Mark Hagen.

In 2017, Bruce was the first recipient of the Full Sail University Industry Icon Award, which is presented annually to individuals who have dedicated their lives to entertainment, media, and the arts, and who have continually given back to Full Sail. He was honored to receive this award and it sits proudly alongside the many other awards he received.

• • •

On Thursday, June 25th, 2009, Michael was found in a coma at his home in Bel Air. Paramedics arrived and he was taken to UCLA Medical Center. In a few hours he was dead.

Roberta had seen the news report online and called us. We were absolutely shocked, shattered. It was impossible to process. The phone started ringing. Everyone was calling: musicians, studio people, family, friends, all wanting to know what happened. We had no idea. No one in the "inner circle" knew any more than anyone else. Websites were overloaded, news sites had outages, Twitter crashed. Fans and press were gathering outside the hospital. We turned on the TV and were glued to CNN. "The King of Pop has died. A very, very sad moment," said anchorman Wolf Blitzer. We just stared at each other, speechless. The whole world was in shock and disbelief at the news. Michael was only fifty years old.

The day before, he had been dancing and singing in rehearsal at the Staples Center in LA, getting ready for his "This is It" shows in London. It was an incredible production and Michael was raring to go. They made an amazing film of the rehearsal footage. He was in full form. Impossible to believe he would be gone the next day.

Insomnia plagued Michael. His personal doctor, Conrad Murray, was at Michael's house and administered a few different medications so he could sleep. Apparently nothing was working. So the doctor gave him a cocktail of the surgical anesthetic Propofol mixed with the sedative Lorazepam. He left the room.

Michael never woke up.

When these details started coming out, we were mad. Everyone was mad. How could that happen? Who is this doctor? We were in shock, we were grieving and we were angry.

Two years later Conrad Murray would be convicted of involuntary manslaughter. Four years in prison was all he got. There were rumors that other people were involved and that Michael had been murdered. Will we ever know the truth?

The memorial service was held, fittingly, in the Staples Center. It was broadcast all over the world. We didn't go. It was too emotional. Thousands were there. It was star-studded, of course. Elizabeth Taylor, Quincy, Rev. Al Sharpton, Macaulay Culkin, Mariah Carey, Stevie Wonder, Gladys Knight, Lionel Richie, Magic Johnson, musicians, dancers, family, friends, and fans. His music was performed and the whole service was done with so much love. "Do it with love, L-O-V-E," he always said.

CNN wanted Bruce to do an interview with Don Lemon. He went to Orlando to do the taping. Don asked him about working with Michael. Bruce said, *"Michael was the ultimate professional. He also had a wonderful human side to him. He was polite and gentle. In a business where we didn't hear these words too often, when Michael would ask for something he would say "Please," "Thank you," "You're welcome." He was loving and kind. He wasn't the kid next door, I don't mean to imply that. But he was phenomenal to work with. His dedication to the work was total, he always had the lyrics memorized, he'd stay up all night preparing."*

Don Lemon commented that Michael had said that "Have You Seen My Childhood" was his most biographical song. Bruce had his score of "Childhood" with him. He showed it to the camera and said, *"This is typical Michael Jackson. He had inscribed: 'To Bruce Swedien, working with you is complete Love, in the highest sense. I will always care for and love you. Thank you for executing the song that's most important to me. "Childhood." It's a statement I've always wanted to make. Love, Michael.'"*

Bruce continued, *"I have trouble speaking about him in the past tense. It's going to take me a while to get used to that. It doesn't seem like he's gone."*

Ironically, Bruce's second book, *In the Studio with Michael Jackson*, would come out later that same month. It was the story of his years working with Michael from *The Wiz* to *Invincible*. On the cover was that iconic photo of Quincy, Bruce, and Michael. It was suddenly so sad. A heavy heart accompanied that book. It became an homage; a tribute. But it is full of the energy of the work they did. Technical details abound, along with stories about Michael and the magic they created together.

Herbie Hancock called Michael's death an "unbelievable tragedy" and wrote: "*Michael was one of the most diligent creators. His passion flowed through every pore of his being. His sense of invention was unparalleled. Who else could have thought of the moonwalk and who else could have created such a unique sense of movement in dance? His contribution to music and music videos; Off the Wall, Thriller, We are the World, are expressions of his consummate talent. Above all his compassion for serving humanity and desire to uplift and encourage excellence are etched in his legacy. He changed the world.*"

• • •

Three of Michael's fans in Paris—Yannick Thiry, Phillipe Zerafa, and Christophe Petitclerc—realized they had one dream in common: meeting Bruce Swedien. So in 2009 they decided to form a not-for-profit organization and called it "Music First." Their first project was to bring Bruce and me to France. We flew to Paris a year later and Bruce spoke (through a translator) to this wonderful group of Michael fans. They were so sincere. We had a wonderful time and met many true music-appreciating people who are still friends to this day. They shared their beautiful city with us. Great food too, needless to say!

• • •

Under the Red Blanket was published in 2011. It was so exciting to have our incredible India story finally in print with great photos, ready to share with the world. It was a unique story, to be sure, and people loved it. I even appeared on a local TV cooking show to promote the book and cook my chicken curry!

My first book about my life growing up in India

Speaking of books, there was another one around the corner for Bruce. Author, recording engineer and musician Bill Gibson called Bruce and told him about The Legacy Series for Hal Leonard Publishing. He had just finished a huge book with Quincy, *On Producing*, and he wanted to work on a book with Bruce too, which would be titled *The Bruce Swedien Recording Method*. Bill came to Ocala and stayed with us. He is the sweetest guy you could imagine and was so easy to have around the studio and the house. Those guys worked tirelessly on this book and the result was worthy of the word "legacy."

• • •

Toward the end of 2011, Siedah Garrett and her fiancé Erik Nuri, manager and former VP at RCA Records, flew out to Ocala to be in, as she put it, "the presence of recording greatness." *"Bruce Swedien was the consummate recording engineer,"* she says. *"I trusted his musical and lyrical ear with all recording decisions. He always had great* musical ideas and fostered a creative and multi-collaborative vibe in the studio. One day, when we were recording background vocals, he shared with me that he's only recorded a handful of people capable of recording a vocal, then have the ability to identically double that vocal, immediately; Michael Jackson, Barbra Streisand, Patti Austin, and yours truly!

I had recorded several songs in LA in preparation to release a new solo album, and I insisted that Bruce be the mix engineer on the most important songs. One of those songs was "Keep On Lovin' You," which was my answer to Michael Jackson for our duet, "I Just Can't Stop Loving You," which Bruce also had mixed on MJ's Bad album. I had written the song because I realized that there were things I had always wanted to say to Michael, but never really had the chance to. So, I put it in a song of appreciation to him.

Once we started in Bruce's studio, I realized that, with his engineering skills and superior microphones, he probably would be able to record a much better lead vocal on me. We re-recorded my lead vocal in the afternoon, and Bruce immediately proceeded to set up the mix. He left the mix on the board overnight, and then the next day together we tweaked it to our satisfaction. We then sent a copy of the mix to my producer back in LA, Dapo Torimiro, who responded with few comments about the level of the low bass frequencies, then gave his approval of the new vocal.

The other songs on which I re-recorded my lead vocals with Bruce were entitled "Ordinary Miracle," and "Answer's Always Love." For those two songs, we invited writer/producer Barry Eastmond to fly down from New York to produce my vocals and approve the mixes. He, too, is a huge fan of Bruce's, and considered it a once-in-a-lifetime opportunity to collaborate on a project with the legendary Bruce Swedien. We had recorded a small gospel choir in New York for the track"Ordinary Miracle," but when Bruce mixed the song, he added his outboard gear to the background vocals with a special setting that made them sound as if there were four times as many voices on the tape.

Throughout the four days of working with Bruce, Bea would stop in to bring us goodies, especially Bruce's favorite popsicles, and to share some of her recollections of Michael Jackson, and of living in Los Angeles. Occasionally we would take breaks to pet the horses and collect eggs laid by the chickens, or ride around the property with Bruce driving the golf cart."

Dear friends Siedah Garrett and Erik Nuri

We loved having Siedah and Erik here. Bruce had her surrounded in Tube Traps (an acoustical room treatment), singing her magic into his special microphones. For those who don't know, Siedah is a virtuoso with the knitting needles too, turning out gorgeous, colorful creations one after another. So when she wasn't recording, she was knitting! We had such a wonderful time together remembering the old days in the studio with Michael and Quincy and the gang.

• • •

Later that year we went back to Minneapolis for a visit. "Godfather of Twin City Music Returns" was the newspaper headline. We went to the old studio, now Creation Audio, owned by Steve Wiese, and had such a wonderful time. There were local musicians and music students asking questions. Herb Pilhofer was there. It was like being in a time machine, a real trip down memory lane. There we were, back in the old studio and still there, glued to the ceiling—after 60 years—were our egg cartons. Bruce told the group they were a "superb and very cheap acoustical treatment." Then he pointed to the four-inch doors. "I built those doors," he said. "If you look carefully at them, you'll see they're very solid, very thick... This place is unbelievable. My whole life started here."

We are so proud of the fact that through all of these decades it has remained a working studio. Steve has done so well with it over the years and they are busy making quality music every day.

Still a great studio! Note the doors that Bruce built.

Our egg cartons are still there today—a little crumbly but they do the job

Bruce and Steve trade studio stories

During our visit they decided to do a recording session in "the house that Bruce built" and Steve brought in singer and pianist Jeanne Arland Peterson, 91, her son Billy, who plays bass, and her daughter, singer

Patty. Bruce had recorded Jeanne in that studio in 1954! This time they did "The Shadow of Your Smile."

Bruce was having fun and joked over the talkback mic, "Patty, just sing it Acapulco!" After recording five tunes, he and the Petersons listened to the playbacks. "Jeanne, you have a real future," he said. She replied, "Well, thank you."

• • •

2012 was the twenty-fifth anniversary of *Bad*. Spike Lee decided to make a documentary to celebrate Michael and that amazing album. He came to our home in Ocala to interview Bruce. (This is no small task: a flight to Orlando, then a two-hour drive to sleepy, horsey Ocala.) Once here, he and Bruce spent hours in the studio talking about Michael and Quincy and *Bad*. Watching this film we were so proud to have known and worked with Michael all those years. And to have loved him and been loved by him. It ends with Michael's riveting, mind-blowing, tear-jerking performance of "Man in the Mirror" live in LA in 1989. That alone said it all. Michael was, and will always be, the greatest.

• • •

Bruce telling the Swedish press that he played all his recordings for me
when he got home from the studio

We celebrated our diamond wedding anniversary in 2013. Sixty years!

Roberta got together with British film editor Gareth Maynard and made a video of 90 greetings from family and friends around the world. Erik Nuri played, Siedah sang, Jack and Bridget Morton created a puppet show, Chuck Wild played the piano, people wrote poems, Ken Nordine sent in an abstract little film of words and music, and there were many beautiful words of congratulations from Sweden, Norway, England, Cuba, Spain, India and of course the U.S. We were so touched because many of them said our marriage was an inspiration to them.

It ended with Quincy saying, *"With every drop of energy in my soul and in the cells of my body, I wish you two a celebration of the happiest day that you ever had in your life. It's amazing. You guys have been married sixty years. That's longer than my three marriages put together! And the beautiful thing about it is the Lord gave you each other and that's a serious blessing. I love you guys from the bottom of my heart."*

· · ·

In 2013 we found ourselves on a long and bumpy flight to Dubai, United Arab Emirates. Yes, it was luxurious first class, but it was a very scary trip. Never before had we experienced turbulence like this. The plane was shaking so badly we thought the bolts were going to shake loose. But we got there in one piece for the Dubai Music Week featuring the Michael Jackson Dream Team: Quincy, Bruce, and Rod. Also speaking and performing were Siedah, Greg Phillinganes, Timbaland, Will.i.am, and Selena Gomez; Ben Fong-Torres of *Rolling Stone* emceed. It was great fun as usual, just with a lot more bling. A lot! We stayed at the Zabeel Saray hotel on the Persian Gulf beach. The opulence was unlike anything I had ever seen before. Everything was gold and gleaming marble. We were treated like royalty. Mostly. The venue was the Dubai World Trade Center. There were more than a few snags in the organization of this event. For one thing, we were kept waiting at the designated door as we tried to get in to do the show, but because of a glitch in communication they wouldn't let us in the building. When it was over we all said, "Goodbye Dubai!"

• • •

I'll never forget the Audio Engineering Society convention at the Jacob Javits Center in New York a month later. This was a huge exposition of thousands of audio professionals and equipment exhibitors from around the world. Bruce couldn't go two feet without someone stopping him and thanking him for his work and artistic influence. He gave a talk called "Bruce Swedien: I Have No Secrets," moderated by Bill Gibson. The hall was packed, standing room only. He shared everything he knew, autographed books, and tirelessly greeted his fans. Since Bruce's work was done in the studio, he rarely got the chance to see the effect the music had on people. It was special for him to meet his fans and hear their stories, to know that he had touched their lives. And for me it was such a thrill to be out and about with him and watching the crowds wait in line to shake his hand and say a few words about how his work had affected their lives. It never got old.

Bruce at AES in New York with fans lining up to meet him

We stayed at the Drake Hotel and it was such a joy to be back in New York! We had many New York memories: the Grammy Awards were held in New York in 1988 when Bruce won for *Bad*; the *HIStory* album and all the projects at Eddie Germano's fabulous studio The Hit Factory. I have loved New York since I was a kid; it was our port out when we came home on those long journeys to and from India. As much as we loved India, the sight of the Statue of Liberty from the deck of the ship always brought tears to our eyes.

The next day Bruce received the APRS Sound Fellowship Award for his "outstanding contribution to the art, science and industry of sound recording." Sir George Martin, of Beatles fame, was the president of the Association of Professional Recording Services, which was based in the U.K. The actual event had happened in London the day before, so they sent representatives to New York to meet Bruce and present his award. As always, he was humble, grateful and honored.

• • •

We both turned 80 in 2014. We had a big party and just carried on carrying on. No big deal. What was a big deal was when Bruce was trying to help our 180-pound dog Boo up onto the bed and fell backwards and broke his hip. Poor guy. But had he landed a few inches further, he would have cracked his head on a big glass coffee table, so it could have been a lot worse. He had surgery and ended up in a wheelchair.

That didn't stop him, of course. We flew to LA, wheelchair and all, for Siedah and Erik's wedding. A beautiful couple, they both really appreciated our coming. They have always been dear friends and we couldn't miss it! It was a beautiful sunset ceremony at TV producer Jeff Franklin's estate in Beverly Hills, high in the hills with stunning vista views. Quincy gave her away. It was so touching.

There are times in this mad world of record making that are so warm and human and real. From the outside, people see the glitz and the glam and think that is it. But what they don't see are the times like this beautiful wedding, with sweet friends all around wishing the very best with all their hearts. Quincy's gang of musicians was like that: A true loving family.

The Dynamic Duo
(Photo credit: Maury Phillips/Getty Images)

We flew back to LA again the next year when Bruce won the "Pensado Giant Award—An Icon in the Industry." The event was held outdoors, under the stars at the Sony Movie lot in Los Angeles, and the award was presented by Quincy, with Siedah, Patti Austin, and Ed Cherney, to a cheering crowd and many standing ovations. Ed narrated a beautiful film they had made about Bruce, calling him "arguably the greatest recording engineer ever." In the film Ed talked about Bruce's career and also described the veritable menagerie of horses, dogs, cats, and chickens at home. There were lovely photos of the two of us over the years. Bruce and Quincy quipped back and forth onstage, calling each other "Jones" and "Svensk." Bruce thanked me from the stage, having me stand up and acknowledge the audience's applause. His appreciation of me and our life together was always there. It was wonderful to be back in LA and see everyone. We spent the afternoons on the terrace of the hotel, sitting in the sun, reminiscing and laughing with friends from the good old studio days.

Quincy and Bruce at the Pensado Awards
(Photo credit: Maury Phillips/Getty Images)

• • •

We lost dear Rod Temperton the next year to lung cancer. Those four packs a day had caught up with him. He was only 66. Kathy was bereft, of course—it's so hard to lose your partner. He was such a great guy and such a talent! He, Bruce, and Quincy were dubbed "The A Team" and worked together on *Off the Wall*, *Thriller*, *Night Shift*, *The Dude*, and lots of other projects.

The BBC paid tribute to him this way: "Apart from Lennon and McCartney, no one from the UK has written more gold plated songs than Rod Temperton. . . a huge loss. RIP."

• • •

Roberta recorded her album *Nordic Miniatures: Now and Then* in our home studio in 2017. It provided a rich variety of music for piano from Denmark, Sweden, Norway, Finland, and Iceland. She commissioned a piece by composers from each country and, influenced by Ken Nordine from the Chicago years, recorded original spoken word tracks in between the music. Ryan Williams was at the helm with Bruce, who, of course, loved Scandinavian music. And he loved her playing. He would always say, "Boy, she can really play!" The musical lineage from his parents to her always moved him.

• • •

We continued having fun. Our energy together never ebbed even as our bodies got older. Bruce loved to swim and was in the pool almost every evening. Friends visited, relatives from Sweden crossed the Atlantic and stayed with us, dinner parties were frequent and filled with joy. We were down to one horse and two dogs, plus some cats and chickens. Our Danes were Tara and Gino, sweet rescues from the amazing Great Dane Love Central Florida. The menagerie was smaller but just as lively and rewarding as ever. Every morning I'd feed and water Angel, the Appaloosa rescue horse, walk her out to the pasture, muck out her stall, throw in fresh shavings, haul the wheelbarrow into the woods, feed and water the chickens, and collect eggs for our breakfast.

Bruce talking about his microphone collection,
holding his classic Neumann U 47

Bruce went to his studio every day. He'd fire up the gear and play tracks for musicians and friends who came by to record or just visit. One of his favorite pieces of music to play was the recording of Joe Williams with the Count Basie band that he engineered at Universal back in 1960. Pure sixty-year old analog: no click track, nothing digital. Just killer musicians playing into microphones, rolling onto tape, engineered/crafted by Bruce.

He loved talking on the phone with old friends and he loved the internet. His curiosity never ebbed; he was always learning, discovering, and enjoying new things.

We loved movies too. Every night after dinner, Bruce would say, "To the movies!" Over 600 films in various formats filled the shelves in our screening room. Michael had given us our first projector and I still sit in the relaxing massage chair he gave us one Christmas years ago.

And we loved food. Food was a serious part of Bruce and Quincy's relationship and ours as well. Bruce's girth was a testimony to that. His birthday favorite was Swedish meatballs, mashed potatoes, and lingonberries. I don't know why, but it took me over twenty years to get him to eat Indian food. Finally he tried it and everything changed. Wherever we lived we became regulars at the local Indian restaurant. Chicken Tikka Masala was his favorite. I have to say, I really wish I had gotten Bruce to go to India, especially up to Nagaland to see the beautiful hills where I grew up, and to meet the warm and welcoming Naga people. I so wanted to share that with him.

• • •

On November 16, 2020, Bruce passed away at the age of eighty-six. He had fallen again, there were problems with the surgery, he got sepsis and Covid, and after a long and difficult hospital stay, his body said *that's enough.*

Bill Gibson wrote the obituary. There were calls and messages from around the world. So many people wrote beautiful tributes. The media lauded Bruce in print and broadcast. National Public Radio announced his passing with the "Billie Jean" track playing in the background. There were articles in the New York Times, BBC, Rolling Stone, the Guardian, LA Times, Variety, Billboard, Svenska Dagbladet, and the Arabic international newspaper Asharq Al-Awsat. We honestly hadn't realized he was that famous.

The Michael Jackson Estate wrote: "*As one of the most imaginative audio engineers to ever enter a recording studio, Bruce Swedien was involved in the creation of some of the most memorable moments for music's most iconic artists. His contribution to Michael Jackson's sound was invaluable, earning him Grammys for the* Thriller, Bad *and* Dangerous *albums. Moreover, Bruce's professional collaboration with Michael became a close friendship they both cherished. Bruce was a kind, generous soul who as he grew older continued to share his knowledge of his craft with younger generations. He will be missed by all whose lives and careers he touched.*"

Ryan Williams wrote: "*Bruce was instrumental in pushing recorded music forward throughout his career. He was an advocate for stereo recording when mono was king; breaking the rules, discovering new and interesting sonic landscapes and always on the forefront of recording technology. His life in the studio is really the story of American popular music. From Count Basie to Jennifer Lopez and everything in between. He saw it all. Rock n Roll, The Blues, RnB, Jazz, you name it. What a perfect time for Bruce to have come along. Right on the cusp of modern popular music and the birth of record making.*"

• • •

Best friends

It's hard to explain losing your husband of almost 68 years. From the little boy who knew me in the womb to the legendary engineer who put his signature on the sound of American music, Bruce was my constant companion. In many ways, he took me along for the ride. In other ways, I made the ride possible for him and us. He thrived on my wildness, my ability to roll with any punches, to keep my cool in any situation, whether it was a tiger outside the tent, hopping from home to home with three children and a veritable menagerie in tow, or hanging in the studio with some of the music industry's biggest celebrities. It didn't matter where we went, as long as we were together.

Carrying on without him has been the most difficult thing I have ever had to do. I miss him every minute of every day. But the memories keep me going. We had such a great life together. Every day was a new adventure.

Of course, all things must pass. But perhaps our love story doesn't have to end. Maybe, wherever there are people falling in love to the music Bruce helped make, our story will go on.

Acknowledgments

My deepest gratitude goes to the late, great Quincy Jones. He made our life together something miraculous and he always made me feel like a welcome member of the family. A more sincere, loving, respectful and brilliant human being you could not imagine.

And to the late, dear sweet Michael Jackson who was love personified. His drive towards perfection in his art changed all of us; we rose to his ideals and were better for it. We had a warm, special friendship for many years.

To our parents, Bengt and Edna Anderson and Ellsworth and Louise Swedien who showed us the joys of adventure, courage, laughter and good food. We couldn't have done this without their help and support.

To the true-blue people who, with their love and encouragement, helped me write this bit of history: Siedah Garrett and Erik Nuri, The Michael Jackson Estate, Matt Forger, Sérgio and Gracinha Mendes, Kathy Buckley, Rod Temperton, Greg Phillinganes, Ed Eckstein, Brian Vibberts, Karen Kittleson, John Robinson, Ryan Williams, Tina Jones, Bjorn Asplind, Steve Wiese, Herb Pilhofer, Ricky Peterson, Bill Gibson, Chuck Wild, Joe Vogel, Craig Anderton, Adam Fell, Arnold Robinson, Alyssa Lein Bryant, Mark Hagen, Bill Putnam Jr., Gareth Maynard, Judy Kelley, Laura Davis, Michael Sainato, Matthew Allen, Niels-Erik Lund, Mickey and Randy Short, Brooke Wentz, Michael Tan, Mark and Mary Emery, Brenda Hudson, Ravi Hutheesing, John Van Nest and many others.

And to the myriad of friends and family that we have known and loved over the years, I also send my sincerest gratitude. So many of you told me again and again to write down these special stories. I'm glad I did.

Index

"2Bad", 142
A&M Records, 114
A&R Studios, 83, 115
ABBA, 140
Abbey Road (album), 62
Academy Awards, 120
Acklin, Barbara, 68
Acoustic Sciences, 175
Acusonic Recording Process, 75
Adams, Chris, 154
AES (Audio Engineering
    Society), 90, 186, 187
Affleck, Ben, 170
"All Time High", 118
Allansson, Leif, 121, 140
Allansson, Margareta, 121, 140
Allen Zentz (recording studio), 85
Allen, Matthew, 73
Alpert, Herb, 114, 118
American Music Awards, 134
An American Werewolf in London
    (film), 110
Anderson Theological College,
    156
Anderson, Audrey, 3, 5, 155, 156,
    171
Anderson, Bengt, 2, 98, 155
Anderson, Bruce, 3, 12, 13, 14,
    17, 18, 20, 22, 23
Anderson, Edna, 2, 156
Anderson, Jim, 2, 5, 12, 17, 18,
    22, 86, 91, 137, 138, 139, 153,
    155, 171
Anderson, June, 3, 5, 17, 22, 171,
    176
Anderson, Stu, 26
Andersson, Benny, 140
Anderton, Craig, 62

"Answer's Always Love", 180
Ao tribe, 4, 6
APRS (Association of
    Professional Recording
    Services), 187
Art Blakey and the Jazz
    Messengers, 27, 74
Ash, Rick, 87
Ashford and Simpson, 79
Asplind, Bjorn, 121, 162, 163
Asplind, Linn, 162, 163
Astoria Studios, 82
Austin, Dallas, 142
Austin, Patti, 77, 79, 88, 90, 91,
    93, 103, 154, 180, 189
"Baby Be Mine", 104
"Baby Come to Me", 77
Babyface, 154
Bacharach, Burt, 103
"Back On The Block", 130, 131
Back on the Block (album), 42,
    129, 130, 158
Backus, Earl, 50
Bad (album), v, 121, 122, 123,
    124, 125, 127, 128, 180, 184,
    187, 193
Bad Luck Is All I Have (album),
    69
Bähler, Michael, 92
Bähler, Tom, 83, 91
Baker, Ginger, 53
Baker, Josephine, 159
Ballard, Glen, 122
Battle, Kathleen, 158
Baum, Frank, 81
Bayer Sager, Carol, 95, 103
Baylor, Tom, 95
"Baywatch" (television series), 98

"Beat It", 106, 108, 119
Beautiful Zion Choir, 43
Belafonte, Harry, 172
Benson, George, 74, 77, 88, 129
Berenson, Berry, 84
Bergman, Alan, 103
Bergman, Marilyn, 103
Bernstein, Leonard, 73
Big-Daddy Kane, 130
"Big Girls Don't Cry", 43
Billboard Music Awards, 134
"Billie Jean", i, 77, 104, 107, 108, 193
Bishop, Joey, 66
Blakey, Art, 68
Blakkestad, Bill, 26
Blam (album), 79, 172
Blitzer, Wolf, 176
Blow Your Own Horn (album), 115
Blumlein Pair, 122
Boddicker, Michael, 88, 91, 95
Boddiker, Michael, 142
Bono, 154
"Boom Boom", 66
"Boston Public" (television series), 80
Bottrell, Bill, 132
Boulanger, Nadia, 73
Braaten, Trond, 164
Brando, Marlon, 124
Brando, Miko, 124
Brandy, 154
Brasileiro (album), 139
Brennan, Walter, 95
Brothers Johnson, i, 75, 77, 79, 91, 146, 172
Brown, James, 146
Brown, Les, 68
Bruce, Jack, 53
Brunswick Records, 48, 67, 68
Bryson, Peabo, 115
Buck, Pearl, 14
Buckley, Francis, 154
"Burn This Disco Out", 86
Butler, Jerry, 46, 70

Buttons, Red, 100
Buxer, Brad, 142, 144
Cahn, Sammy, 102
Caine, Michael, 100, 129
Campbell, Naomi, 100
Cannon, Dyan, 100, 103
Capitol Records, 66
Capone, Al, 158
Cardona, Javier, 150, 153
Cardona, Maricela, 150, 153
Carey, Mariah, 177
Carter, Ron, 75
Chandler, Gene, 67, 68
Chaplin, Charlie, 115, 143
Charles, Ray, 46, 74, 76, 100, 129, 154
Cherney, Ed, 64, 65, 92, 108, 175, 189
Cherokee (recording studio), 85, 87
Chicago Conservatory of Music, iii, 54
Chicago Symphony Orchestra, iii, 33, 34, 35, 36, 58, 68, 142
Chi-Lites, 65, 67, 68
Clapper, Bernie, 39
Clapton, Eric, 53
Cole, Nat King, 159
Cole, Natalie, 66
Collins, Jackie, 102
Collins, Phil, 154
Colors (album), 57
Como Ama una Mujer (album), 170
Confetti (album), 115
Conger, Steve, 87
Cooke, Sam, 46
Coolidge, Rita, 118
Copland, Aaron, 73
Corea, Chick, 158
Costa, Don, 48
Count Basie Band, i, 41, 42, 68, 74, 192, 193
Cream (group), 53
Creation Audio, 24, 181
Cross, Christopher, 103

Crouch, Andraé, 43, 122, 123
Crystal, Billy, 121
Culkin, Macaulay, 133, 162, 177
da Costa, Paulhino, 76, 86, 91
"Dangerous", 133
Dangerous (album), 122, 132, 133, 134, 135, 193
Davis Jr., Sammy, 66
Davis, Carl, 67, 70
Davis, Miles, 101, 129, 154
Davis, Tyrone, 67, 68
De Niro, Robert, 102
Dietrich, Marlene, 158
"Do You Love What You Feel", 77
Dorsey, Jimmy, 23, 68
Dorsey, Tommy, 23, 68
Dove (book), 129
Downs, Bill, 29
Downs, Fred, 128
Downs, Jane, 128
"Duke of Earl", 67
Dukes of Dixieland, The, 33
Dylan, Bob, 65
E.T.-The Extra-Terrestrial (album), 103
Earth, Wind & Fire, 170
Eastmond, Barry, 180
Eckstine, Billy, 154
Eckstine, Ed, 94
Edna Anderson Garden, 156
EGREM (recording studio), 159
Electronic Concept Orchestra, 61
Ellington, Duke, vi, 40, 43, 68, 74
Emmy Award, 79
Epic Records, 109
Evans, Dale, 63
Feldman, Marty, 62, 63, 64
Fisher, Carrie, 102
Fitzgerald, Ella, 129
Flack, Roberta, 75, 103, 115
Flickinger, Daniel, 63
Flockhart, Calista, 100
Fong-Torres, Ben, 186
Ford, Harrison, 100, 140
Ford, Phil, 42

Forger, Matt, 107, 109, 142
Frankie Valli and the Four Seasons, 43, 68
Franklin, Jeff, 188
*Free Willy (*film), 135
Frigo, Johnny, 50
Full Sail University, 175
Gable, Clark, 139
Gadd, Steve, 79
Gallin, Sandy, 133, 134
Gardner, Brian, 91
Garrett, Siedah, 121, 122, 129, 140, 154, 179, 181, 185, 186, 188, 189
Germano, Eddie, 142, 187
Gershwin, George, 158
Gershwin, Ira, 158
Gershwin's World (album), 158
Gibb, Maurice, 100
Gibson, Bill, 179, 186, 192
Gillespie, Dizzy, 74, 129, 154
"Give Me the Night", 77
Goldberg, Whoopi, 102
Gomez, Selena, 186
Goodell, John, 11
Gore, Lesley, 70
Grammy Award, 33, 40, 42, 43, 48, 61, 62, 66, 67, 74, 76, 80, 87, 92, 94, 103, 111, 112, 128, 129, 131, 134, 139, 154, 158, 166, 187, 193
Groove (album), 61
Grundman, Bernie, 91, 109, 140, 154, 175
Grundman, Claire, 140, 154
Grusin, Dave, 70
Gruyer, Jean, 66
Hagen, Mark, 123
Haley, Alex, 79
Hampton, Lionel, 68, 74
Hampton, Riley, 46
Hancock, Herbie, 68, 70, 75, 79, 88, 92, 158, 178
Hanrahan, Kevin, 158
Harrah, Bill, 102
Harrah, Verna, 101, 128

Harris, Eddie, 27, 62, 63, 69, 70
Harris, Sally, 69, 70
Hasselhoff, David, 98, 99
"Have You Seen Her", 67
"Have You Seen My Childhood",
    143, 144, 177
"Heal the World", 133
Hefner, Hugh, 48
Herman, Woody, 68
Herseth, Adolph 'Bud', 34
Hey, Jerry, 76, 86, 88, 91, 121,
    131
Higgins, Eddie, 61
Hines, Gregory, 121
Hines, Mimi, 42
HIStory Past, Present and Future
    (album), 140, 142, 144, 149,
    187
Hit Factory, 142, 144, 145, 146,
    154, 160, 187
Hoffman, Dustin, 153
Holiday, Billie, 74
Holiday, Jennifer, 129
Hooker, John Lee, 66, 68
Hormel, Geordie, 25, 27, 69
Horne, Lena, v, 65, 82, 83, 94,
    100, 124
Houston, Cissy, 75
"How Can You Live Like That",
    69
Howard, Ron, 103
"Human Nature", 104
"I Just Can't Stop Loving You",
    180
"I Need Some Money", 69
I'm the One (album), 103
Ice-T, 130
"In the Studio with Bruce
    Swedien" master class, 174
Ingram, James, 76, 77, 91, 103,
    129, 130
Inseparable (album), 66
Invincible (album), 160, 177
"It's My Party", 70
Jackson 5, 115
Jackson, Katherine, 162

Jackson, Michael, v, vi, 65, 67,
    74, 75, 76, 77, 82, 93, 100,
    103, 104, 106, 107, 108, 109,
    110, 111, 113, 114, 115, 116,
    117, 118, 119, 120, 121, 122,
    123, 124, 125, 126, 127, 129,
    132, 133, 134, 140, 141, 142,
    143, 144, 145, 146, 147, 149,
    150, 153, 160, 161, 162, 163,
    176, 177, 178, 180, 181, 184,
    186, 192, 193
Jackson, Paris, 160
Jackson, Prince, 160
Jagger, Mick, vi, 115, 116
"Jam", 133, 134
James, Bob, 75
Janis, Johnny, 48, 68
Jarreau, Al, 130
Jennings, John, 175
Johnson, Craig, 142
Johnson, Louis, 75, 86, 88, 91
Johnson, Magic, 177
Jones, Garry, 175
Jones, Jazz, 74
Jones, Jolie, 129
Jones, Kidada, 80, 97, 100, 101,
    129
Jones, Quincy, vi, 22, 40, 42, 43,
    65, 70, 72, 73, 74, 75, 77, 78,
    79, 80, 81, 83, 84, 85, 86, 88,
    89, 90, 91, 93, 94, 95, 97, 98,
    100, 101, 102, 103, 104, 105,
    106, 107, 109, 113, 120, 121,
    122, 124, 125, 126, 127, 128,
    129, 130, 131, 132, 154, 158,
    172, 177, 179, 181, 184, 185,
    186, 188, 189, 190, 192
Jones, Quincy III, 73, 124, 126,
    127, 129, 130
Jones, Rashida, 80, 97, 129
Jones, Tina, 97, 129
Jones: The Many Lives of Q
    (documentary), 75
Jook Joint (album), 154
Juarez, Julio, 113, 114
"Just Once", 76, 91

Just the Blues (album), 41
Kaiser, Kurt, 44
Kantola, Martin, 175
Karr, Dave, 26
Kayden, Jerold, 124
Keaton, Michael, 103
"Keep the Faith", 122
Kelley, Judy, 115, 139, 150
Kendun Studios, 88, 89
Kenton, Stan, 68
Khan, Chaka, 65, 74, 75, 79, 88, 91, 103, 129, 154
Kimberly, Jim, 50
Kissinger, Henry, 153
Kittleson, Karen, 88, 91
Klett, John, 175
Knight, Gladys, 177
"Knight Rider" (television series), 99
"Kojak" (television series), 81
Kool Mo-Dee, 130
Landgren, Nils, 140
Larrabee Studios, 133
Lawford, Peter, 66
Laws, Hubert, 75, 79
Layton, Lewis, 33
Lean, David, 153
Lean, Sandy, 153
"Leave Me Alone", 128
Lee, Spike, 184
Lemon, Don, 177
Levin, Andres, 160
Levin, Ileana, 160
Levine, Andres, 158, 159
Lewis, Emanuel, 100
Lewis, Jerry, 18
Lewis, Ramsey, 48
Light Up The Night (album), 79
Lindstrom, Per, 118
Link, Richard, 26
Lipton, Peggy, 80, 97, 103, 104
Live at Mr. Kelly's (album), 66
LL Cool J, 129
Loggins, Kenny, 103
Lohr, Bernard, 140
Lohr, Ulli, 140

Lombard, Carol, 139
London, Julie, 68
Lonesome Dove (film), 135
Lopez, Jennifer, vi, 168, 169, 170, 193
Love Me By Name (album), 70
"Love X Love", 88
Lubbock, Jeremy, 143
Luciano, Lucky, 158
Lukather, Steve, 76, 77, 86, 91, 104
Lumet, Sidney, 82, 83, 84
Lund, Annette, 172
Lund, Niels Erik, 79, 172
Mack, James, 68
Make Mine Music (book), 76, 162, 171
"Man in the Mirror", 122, 184
Mancini, Henry, 46
Mann, Herbie, 26, 27, 68
Martin, Dean, 18, 66
Martin, George, 187
Martinez, Cyrius, 158, 159
Marx, Dick, 48, 49, 50, 58, 65, 66
Marx, Richard, 49
Marx, Ruth, 49, 58, 66
Mason, Harvey, 70, 75
Masterjam (album), 91
Matthau, Walter, 153
Max, Peter, 120
Mayfield, Curtis, 46, 68
McBride, Robin, 61
McCartney, Paul, vi, 106, 116, 190
McCrea, Joel, 95
McDonald, Michael, 79, 103, 121
McDonald, Ralph, 75
McFerrin, Bobby, 130
meatballs, swedish, 22, 92, 192
Mechan, Ramsees, 175
Medina, Benny, 169
Melle-Mel, 130
Mendes, Gracinha, 115, 139, 140
Mendes, Sérgio, 115, 139, 140, 155
Mercer, Johnny, 46

Mercury Records, 61, 70
Michael, George, 100, 129
Miles, Buddy, 61, 68
Missing Persons, 120
Mister Kelly's, 39, 49, 67
Mitchell, Joni, 158
"Moody's Mood For Love", 89
Moog, Bob, 61, 62, 63, 64
"Moon River", 46
Moore, Rene, 142
Moore, Roger, 172
Morey, Jim, 133
Morita, Akio, 126
Morton, Bridget, 185
Morton, Jack, 185
Muddy Waters, 66, 68
Murguia, Lupita, 155
Murguia, Ricardo, 155
Murphy, Eddie, 110
Murray, Conrad, 176
Nagaland, vii, 2, 12, 132, 141,
    145, 155, 171, 192
NARAS (National Academy of
    Recording Arts and Science),
    75
Nelson, Willie, 65
"Never Gonna Let You Go", 115
Never on Sunday (album), 48
Neverland, 113, 116, 117, 139
Newton John, Olivia, 172
Nicholson, Jack, 129
Night Shift (film), 103, 190
Nordic Audio Labs, 175
Nordic Miniatures: Now and
    Then (album), 190
Nordine, Beryl, 140
Nordine, Ken, 57, 58, 61, 140,
    185, 190
Now Nordine (radio show), 57
Noxon, Art, 175
Nuri, Erik, 4, 140, 179, 181, 185,
    188
Ocean Way Studios, 131
Octopussy (film), 118
Odin (boat), 46, 54, 59, 99, 119,
    153

"Off the Wall", 86
Off the Wall (album), 65, 76, 83,
    85, 86, 87, 103, 178, 190
"Oh Girl", 67
On Producing (book), 179
"One Hundred Ways", 76, 91
"Ordinary Miracle", 180
Orpheus Chamber Orchestra, 158
Oscar Peterson Trio, 40, 48
Ostin, Evelyn, 100
Ostin, Mo, 100
Padron, Ileana, 159
Page, Patti, 32
Paich, David, 104
Paich, Marty, 89, 90
Panico, Claire, 66
Panico, Frank, 66
Paragon Recording Studios, 62,
    64
Parker, Charlie, 154
"Parks and Recreation"
    (television series), 80
Peck, Gregory, 100
Pensado Awards, 189, 190
Peter, Paul, and Mary, 55
Peterson, Billy, 183
Peterson, Jeanne, 26, 183, 184
Peterson, Oscar, vi, 39, 40, 41,
    48, 68
Peterson, Patty, 184
Petitclerc, Christophe, 178
Phillinganes, Greg, 76, 86, 88, 90,
    91, 95, 121, 124, 154, 186
Pilhofer, Herb, 27, 182
Pittinsky, Scott, 146
Pizullo, Joe, 115
Poitier, Joanna, 101
Poitier, Sidney, 100, 101, 120,
    129
Poledouris, Basil, 135
Poledouris, Bobbie, 135
Presley, Lisa-Marie, 142
Price, Vincent, 104, 105, 106
Prima, Louis, 68
Prince, 110
Pryor, Richard, 82

Putnam, Bill, 31, 32, 37, 109
Q on Producing (book), 77
Quincy Jones Productions, 128
Qwest Records, 94
Raitt, Bonnie, 65
Ravenscroft, Thurl, 51
RCA Studios, 32, 33
Reagan, Nancy, 114, 117
Reagan, Ronald, 114
Rebirth (album*)*, 170
Record One Studios, 140, 141
Record, Eugene, 68
Red Horn (album), 140
Redding, Otis, 46
Reiner, Fritz, 33, 34, 35
"Remember the Time", 133
Rhyme and Reason (album), 120
Richard, Ben, 174
Richie, Lionel, 103, 120, 177
Rickles, Don, 100, 129
Riggi, Charlie, 136
Riggi, Judi, 136
Rikarp, Sven Arne, 56
Riley, Teddy, 132
Robinson, John (JR), 75, 86, 88,
    91, 154
Rock and Roll Hall of Fame, 67
"Rock With You", 76, 86
Rogers, Roy, 63
Rolling Stones, 65
"Roots" (television series), 79
Ross, Diana, 82, 83, 110
Ross, Mark, 124, 128
Ross, Sally, 124, 128
Ross, Steve, 124, 128
Ross, Ted, 82
Roulette Records, 41
Royer Microphones, 175
Rubenstein, Marty, 49
Rufus (band), 74, 75, 77, 88, 91,
    103
Rullo, Frank, 50
Running Scared (film), 121
Russell, Brenda, 103
Russell, Mary Chacko, 15
Russell, Nipsey, 82

Sands, Tommy, 53
Savalas, Telly, 81
"Say, Say, Say", 116
Scheps, Andrew, 142
Schifrin, Lalo, 43
Schmitt Music Company, 23
Schmitt, Al, 154
Scorsese, Martin, 123, 124
Sérgio Mendes (album), 115
Shapey, Ralph, 68
Sharpton, Al, 177
"She's Out of My Life", 83
Shields, Brooke, 97
Shore, Dinah, 68
Short, Mickey, 86, 99, 129, 160
Short, Randy, 86, 99, 129, 160
Shorter, Wayne, 158
Sides, Allen, 131, 140
Sides, Ann, 140
Simon, Paul, 102
Sinatra, Frank, 23, 39, 53, 66
Sinatra, Nancy, 53
Smalls, Charlie, 75
"Smile", 143, 144
Smith, Keely, 68
"Smooth Criminal", 122, 123
Smothers Brothers, 42
Soderblom, Kenny, 50
"Someone in the Dark", 103
Sondheim, Stephen, 153
Sony Records, 133
Sony Studios, 158
Soul Train Music Awards, 134
"Soulful Strut", 48
Sound Market Studios, 65
Sounds and Stuff Like That
    (album), 75, 79, 158, 172
Spielberg, Steven, 93, 103, 120
St. Olaf Choir, 43
"Starlight", 104
"State of Independence", 103
"State of Shock", 115
"Stomp", 77
Stracke, Win, 61
Streisand, Barbra, 2, vi, 100, 128,
    129, 180

sugar cookies, 6, 22, 92
Summer, Donna, 74, 103
Sundberg, Brad, 142
Swedien Recording Studios, 24, 26
Swedien, Bea, i, iii, v, 98, 111, 121, 124, 163, 169, 181
Swedien, Bruce, i, iii, v, vi, 7, 8, 9, 10, 11, 18, 19, 20, 21, 22, 23, 24, 25, 27, 28, 29, 31, 32, 33, 36, 37, 38, 39, 40, 41, 42, 43, 44, 45, 46, 47, 48, 49, 50, 51, 52, 53, 54, 55, 57, 58, 59, 61, 62, 64, 65, 66, 67, 68, 69, 70, 71, 72, 73, 74, 75, 76, 77, 79, 81, 82, 83, 84, 85, 86, 87, 88, 89, 90, 91, 92, 93, 94, 95, 96, 98, 99, 100, 101, 102, 103, 104, 105, 106, 107, 108, 109, 110, 111, 112, 113, 114, 115, 116, 117, 118, 119, 120, 121, 122, 123, 124, 125, 126, 127, 128, 129, 130, 131, 132, 133, 134, 135, 136, 139, 140, 141, 142, 143, 149, 150, 152, 154, 155, 158, 159, 160, 162, 163, 164, 165, 166, 167, 168, 169, 170, 171, 172, 173, 174, 175, 177, 178, 179, 180, 181, 182, 183, 184, 185, 186, 187, 188, 189, 190, 191, 192, 193, 194
Swedien, David, 28, 53, 59
Swedien, Ellsworth, 8, 10
Swedien, Julie, 28
Swedien, Louise, 8, 9, 10
Swedien, Roberta, 15, 21, 28, 37, 49, 53, 54, 61, 68, 86, 118, 134, 137, 138, 139, 144, 155, 157, 158, 160, 162, 164, 165, 166, 176, 185, 190
"Sweet Freedom", 121
Take Six, 129
Tamia, 77
Tarnapol, Carl, 67
Tarnapol, Nat, 67

Taylor, Elizabeth, 100, 129, 162, 177
Temperton, Kathy Buckley, 85, 86, 93, 97, 139, 190
Temperton, Rod, i, 85, 86, 88, 91, 93, 95, 97, 103, 104, 105, 109, 121, 130, 131, 139, 154, 186, 190
Terry, Clark, 74
"That Is Why You're Overweight", 69
The Beatles, 62
The Blue Lagoon (film), 135
The Bruce Swedien Recording Method (book), 179
The Cole Porter Songbook (album), 40
The Color Purple (film), 120
The Dude (album), 65, 76, 91, 190
The Duke Ellington Songbook (album), 40
The Four Aces, 19
The Gershwin Songbook (album), 40
"The Girl Is Mine", 106

The Harold Arlen Songbook (album), 40
The Hunt for Red October (film), 135
The Jerome Kern Songbook (album), 40
"The Lady in My Life", 104
The London House Sessions (album), 40
The Many Lives of Q (documentary), 77
"The Mod Squad" (television series), 80
"The Office" (television series), 80
"The Places You'll Find Love", 129
"The Secret Garden", 77
The Pointer Sisters, 1, 103, 129

"The Reason Why I'm Talking S–T!", 69
The Record Plant, 170
The Richard Rodgers Songbook (album), 40
The Singers Unlimited, 51
The Six Fat Dutchmen, 27
The St. Olaf Choir, 68
The Tijuana Brass, 114
The Village Recorder, 27
The Wiz (film), 74, 75, 81, 82, 83, 84, 85, 94, 177
Them Changes (album), 61
Thielemans, Toots, 70, 154
Thiry, Yannick, 178
This is Me... Then (album), 170
"This Time Around", 142
Thriller (album), i, 67, 77, 103, 105, 106, 107, 109, 110, 112, 113, 115, 121, 128, 178, 190, 193
Till I Loved You (album), 129
Timbaland, 186
Timmons, Bobby, 26
Tomlin, Lily, 95
Torimiro, Dapo, 180
Toto, 2, 76, 77, 104
Tube Traps, 181
"Turn Back the Hands of Time", 67
Turner, Tina, 172
"Twin Peaks" (television series), 80
Tyson, Cicely, 101
Un Nuevo Dia (television series), 155
Under the Red Blanket (book), vi, 171, 178
United Recording, 39
Universal Audio, 109, 110
Universal Recording Studios, iii, 31, 34, 39, 40, 44, 46, 50, 53, 54, 66, 67, 192
Universal Studios, 115
Upchurch, Phil, 70
Van Damme, Art, 55

Van Halen, Eddie, 106
Vandross, Luther, 75, 79, 129
Vaughan, Sarah, 39, 42, 68, 129, 154
Vdovin, Marsha, 109
Vibberts, Brian, 142
Vicari, Tommy, 154
Victory (album), 115
Village Recorder, 69
Wacker, Fred, 50
Wacker, Jana, 50
Wade in the Water (album), 48
Walker, Alice, 120
Walking in Space (album), 76
Warwick, Dionne, 103, 129, 130
Washington, Dinah, vi, 39, 68, 70, 74
"We Are The World", 120
West Viking Studios, 54
Westlake Studios, 85, 93, 108, 109, 120, 123
"What a Diff'rence a Day Makes, 39, 74
White, Barry, 129, 154
White, Maurice, 170
White, Verdine, 170
Widmark, Richard, 153
Wiese, Steve, 24, 181, 182, 183
Wild, Chuck, 120, 140, 185
"Will You Be There?", 135
Will.i.am, 186
Williams, Joe, 192
Williams, John, 103
Williams, Ryan, 174, 191, 193
Wilson, Jackie, 67, 68
Wilson, Nancy, 154
Winfrey, Oprah, 100, 120, 129
Winkler, Henry, 103
Winter, Edgar, 121
Wizard of Oz (book), 81
Wonder, Stevie, 79, 92, 100, 103, 154, 158, 177
Woodstock School, 3, 12, 13, 14, 15, 17, 128, 137, 153
Word Records, 44
"Yah Mo Be There", 77

"You Belong To Me", 170

"You Put a Move On My Heart", 77

"Your Love Keeps Lifting Me Higher", 67

You Are Everything (album), 98

Young-Holt Unlimited, 48

Zawinul, Joe, 130

Zephyr Records, 25

Zerafa, Phillipe, 178